Blessed

is the

Daughter

GOD MAKE THEE LIKE SARAH, REBEKAH, RACHEL, AND LEAH.

Parents thus bless their daughters on the eve of the Sabbath and festivals.

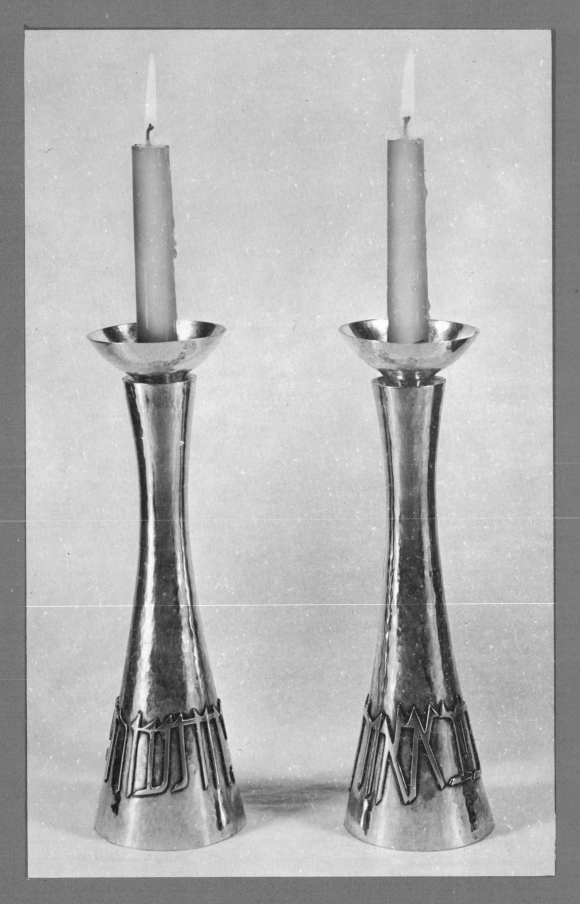

No generation can be redeemed except through the merit of the righteous women of that era.

Midrash

Candlesticks by Ludwig Yehuda Wolpert

Blessed is the Daughter

MEYER WAXMAN

SULAMITH ISH-KISHOR   JACOB SLOAN

FIFTH EDITION

SHENGOLD PUBLISHERS, INC.

New York City

Copyright 1959 by Shengold Publishers, Inc.

New York

All rights reserved

First Edition, November 1959
Second Edition, November 1961
Third Edition, June 1965
Fourth Edition, April 1968
Fifth Edition, August 1971

DESIGNED BY H. FELIX KRAUS
Library of Congress Catalog Card Number: **65-12053**
PRINTED IN THE UNITED STATES OF AMERICA

Contents

Human Freedom • Influence of Passover Story on Liberation Movements Throughout History • *Matzah*—The Unleavened Bread • The *Seder* and the Narration of the *Haggadah* • *Hag he-Aviv*, the Festival of Spring.

LIST OF ILLUSTRATIONS

LIST OF ILLUSTRATIONS

Introduction

In 1955 I published BAR MITZVAH ILLUSTRATED, a compilation for the Jewish boy entering the community of Israel. Many persons were kind enough to praise the impact of the book on the mind and heart of its young readers, and they went so far as to intimate that the feminine counterpart of the bar mitzvah merited a similar literary compendium.

BLESSED IS THE DAUGHTER is an attempt to provide young Jewish girls who have reached the Bat Mitzvah and confirmation period with knowledge and information concerning their people and faith. This volume recounts the entire story of Jewish women's achievement in preserving the sanctities of the past, and their heroism in protecting the Jewish people from the corrosion of ignorance, persecution, and apostasy. It seeks to provide an outline of Jewish life in home and synagogue, after which the reader may fashion her own life as a Jew. The laws of the Sabbath and prayers and festivals are presented in a manner calculated both to interest the reader and to sustain her loyalty. As in the previous volume, many photographs and reproductions have been included to lend significance to the text.

Obviously the subject is so vast that no single volume can begin to exhaust the many ramifications of the contributions of women to Jewry. However, every endeavor has been employed to provide a true picture of the Jewish woman for a wide range of readers. For in that picture there is much exaltation, much brilliance, and courage which will inspire the young Jewish daughters of today.

I wish to acknowledge my indebtedness to all who have contributed to this volume. I am most grateful to Professor Meyer Waxman for his essays on "Jewish Women in Life and Literature" and "Highlights of the History of the Jews"; and to Sulamith Ish-Kishor and Jacob Sloan for their original essays and contributions. The material on the holidays and festivals by Abraham Burstein, and on Jewish observances by Hillel Seidman, appeared first in BAR MITZVAH ILLUSTRATED, edited by Professor A. I. Katsh.

My special thanks to Dr. Stephen S. Kayser, curator of The Jewish Museum, for his constant counsel and aid in choice of illustrative material; to the Hadassah Organization of America for the use of picture and text; to the Zionist archives and Mrs. Sylvia Landress, its director; and to McGraw-Hill Book Company, for permission to reprint a selection from NOTES FROM THE WARSAW GHETTO, edited by Jacob Sloan. My sincere thanks to Bess Myerson for her generous cooperation. I acknowledge with profound gratitude the immeasurable help extended by Mrs. Miriam Messeloff.

Thanks too, to the artists whose works are reproduced in this volume, as well as in BAR MITZVAH ILLUSTRATED. These include Chaim Gross, A. Raymond Katz, Nathan Rappaport, Ilya Schor, Anna Walinska, and Ludwig J. Wolpert.

The aid and cooperation of all these have proved a blessing to the compiler; and may they prove equally beneficial to all who take up the book for enlightenment and guidance.

MOSHE SHEINBAUM

Many daughters have done worthily, but thou excellest them all.

Proverbs

JEWESS, by Anna Walinska

JEWISH WOMEN IN LIFE AND LITERATURE

by Meyer Waxman

According to the Jewish religion, women are just as important human beings as men are. The Bible states this fundamental idea very clearly, in telling the story of God's creation of all life. "Male and female created he them." The same act of creation applied to both man and woman, making them equal from the very beginning. Both were created in the image of God. That is to say, though God first created man, and then took a rib from Adam's side to create Eve, He created both Adam and Eve in the same spirit. Women have as much of the divine spirit in them as men have.

The idea of woman's equality with man is stressed again in still another verse describing the creation of human beings.

"In the day that God created man, in the likeness of God made he him; Male and female created he them; and blessed them, and called their name Adam, in the day when they were created."

The Zohar, the cabalistic Book of Splendor, explains why the Bible uses the plural in referring to Adam:

"The Bible says, 'He blessed *them* and called their name Adam,' not 'He blessed *him* and called his name Adam.' This is intended to show us that God's blessing and the name of Adam belong to both man and woman, equally."

Woman in Biblical Times

From Biblical times to the present, all of Jewish literature has emphasized the value and importance of great women. The long life history of our people is full of examples. The matriarchs, or mothers of the nation, were accorded the same respect down through the ages as were the patriarchs. They are surrounded by a halo of beauty, virtue, and wisdom.

13

"And Sarah heard in the tent door . . . Wherefore did Sarah laugh, saying: Shall I of a surety bear a child, who am old?" — "Is anything too hard for the Lord?" . . . Gen. 18:10, 13, 14

Thus Jewish legend tells us that Sarah was so beautiful that when the casket where Abraham secreted her when they came to Egypt was forced open, her beauty flooded all of Egypt with light. And when Pharaoh, King of Egypt, saw Sarah, he was so enamored of her that he then and there wrote out a marriage contract deeding her all his possessions. Besides, he gave Sarah the province of Goshen — which her descendants later occupied as their rightful property. But most remarkable of all, Pharaoh gave Sarah his own daughter, Hagar, to be her handmaiden; he preferred that Hagar be Sarah's servant rather than another woman's mistress.

The Bible tells us how Rebecca helped her son Jacob secure his father Isaac's greatly desired blessing by deceit. Jewish legend insists that Rebecca was justified, for she was not motivated by a greater love for Jacob, but rather by a deep conviction that Esau was not destined to receive the blessing. So, when Jacob hesitated to follow Rebecca's bidding and win his father's blessing through chicanery, his mother said to him, according to legend: "Do as I bid thee. Obey me, as is thy wont. For thou art my son whose children, every one of them, will be goodly and God-fearing. Not one will be lacking in grace." Obviously, descendants such as these will deserve the blessing that Jacob must obtain for them, even by a ruse.

Rachel, the third of the great matriarchs, was also credited with remarkable virtue. She was said to have warned Jacob of her father, Laban's, intention of substituting her sister, Leah, for her on the wedding night. Rachel and Jacob agreed on a sign by which Jacob might recognize his true love. But when Rachel saw Leah being led into the marriage chamber, she stifled her great love for Jacob so as not to put Leah to shame, and told Leah the sign that had been agreed upon.

The Bible mentions that Rachel was buried on the road to Ephrat. Legend would have it that Jacob had selected this burial place for Rachel. Gifted with the spirit of prophecy, Jacob foresaw that the Judean exiles would pass this point on their march to exile in Babylonia; as they passed by her grave, Rachel would entreat

"And Rebekah lifted up her eyes, and when she saw Isaac, she alighted from
the camel." . . . Gen. 24:64

(Eighteenth century engraving)

the Lord to show her children mercy. That was why the prophet Jeremiah, in one
of his consoling prophecies, sees Rachel in a vision rising from her grave.

And Jacob served seven years for Rachel; and they seemed unto him but
a few days, for the love he had to her" . . . Gen. 29:20

(William Dyce, 1806-64)

"A voice was heard in Ramah, of lamentation and bitter weeping; Rachel weeping for her children; She refuseth to be comforted for her children, because they are not.

"Thus saith the Lord: Refrain thy voice from weeping, and thine eyes from tears: for thy work shall be rewarded, saith the Lord; and they shall come again from the land of the enemy."

THE TOMB OF RACHEL

At the side of Moses, the redeemer of the people of Israel from slavery in Egypt, stood his sister Miriam. She led the women of Israel in song and dance after they crossed the Red Sea miraculously. Part of her song is even incorporated in the Bible. An ancient book records the very day of Miriam's death (it was the 10th day of the month of Sivan). The well of water which accompanied the Jews through the desert from Egypt to the Promised Land of Canaan was obviously to be attributed to Miriam's influence, for the well disappeared at her death.

It is interesting to trace the reasoning behind this legend, so characteristic of how our ancient sages interpreted the Bible to make what they felt was an important point. We read in the Book of Numbers, at the beginning of chapter 20, that Miriam died at Kadesh where she was buried. The Bible continues: "And there was no water for the congregation . . ." Since these two facts—first that Miriam died, and second, that there was no water—follow one another in the Bible, our sages deduced that it was Miriam who had been responsible for the presence of water, which, with her death, disappeared. Miriam was also credited by the Bible with the gift of prophecy; she is called "the prophetess Miriam" (Exodus 15:20).

16

"And Miriam the prophetess, the sister of Aaron, took a timbrel in her hand;
and all the women went out after her with timbrels and with dances. And Miriam
sang unto them" . . . Ex. 15:20-1
(Ninteenth century engraving)

There were other prophetesses whom the Bible describes as accomplishing great
things for their people. Soon after the Hebrew tribes entered the Promised Land
and settled in it, the judge Deborah arose. Fired with the holy spirit, Deborah com-
pletes the conquest of the land which time and circumstances had prevented Joshua
from carrying out. She orders Barak, the chief of the tribes of Naphtali and Zebulun,
to raise an army and liberate a large part of the land that was under the rule of the
most powerful of the Canaanite kings, Yabin. Barak calls on Deborah to accompany
his forces and inspire the troops—the war will be lost without her presence. Deborah
agrees; together with Barak, she leads the tribal army to victory, uniting the entire
country under Jewish rule. In celebration of this triumph, Deborah, a poet as well

17

as judge and prophetess, composed a song of victory. It is found in the Bible, in the fifth chapter of Judges, and is one of the finest heroic poems in world literature. It begins with the stirring verses:

> For that the leaders in Israel led, and the people willingly offered themselves, bless ye the Lord.
>
> Hear, O ye kings; give ear, O ye princes; I, *even* I, will sing unto the Lord; I will sing *praise* to the Lord God of Israel.
>
> Lord, when thou wentest out of Seir, when thou marchedst out of the field of Edom, the earth trembled, and the heavens dropped, the clouds also dropped water.
>
> The mountains melted from before the Lord, *even* that Sinai from before the Lord God of Israel.
>
> In the days of Shamgar the son of Anath, in the days of Jael, the highways were unoccupied, and the travellers walked through byways.
>
> The rulers ceased in Israel, they ceased, until that I Deborah arose, that I arose a mother in Israel.
>
> They chose new gods; then *was* war in the gates: was there a shield or spear seen among forty thousand in Israel?
>
> My heart *is* toward the governors of Israel, that offered themselves willingly among the people. Bless ye the Lord.

SONG OF DEBORAH, by Inbal Dance Theatre
(America—Israel Culture Foundation)

Speak, ye that ride on white asses, ye that sit in judgment, and walk by the way.

Louder than the voice of those who march in rows in the places of drawing water, there shall they rehearse the righteous acts of the Lord, even the righteous acts of his rule in Israel: then shall the people of the Lord go down to the gates.

Awake, awake, Deborah: awake, awake, utter a song: arise, Barak, and lead thy captivity captive, thou son of Abinoam.

Then he made him that remaineth have dominion over the nobles among the people: the Lord made me have dominion over the mighty.

They whose root is out of Ephraim were against Amalek; after thee, Benjamin, among thy people; out of Machir came down governors, and out of Zebulun they that handle the pen of the writer.

And the princes of Issachar *were* with Deborah; even Issachar, and also Barak: he was sent on foot into the valley. For the divisions of Reuben, *there were* great thoughts of heart.

Why abodest thou among the sheepfolds, to hear the bleatings of the flocks? For the divisions of Reuben *there were* great searchings of heart.

JAEL KILLS SISERA

"Blessed above women shall Jael be,
The wife of Heber the Kenite,
Above women in the tent shall she be blessed"
. . . and she hammered Sisera, she struck his head, yea, she pierced and struck
through his temples.
At her feet he bowed, he fell, he lay down . . . Judges 5:24-27

Nor were Miriam and Deborah the only women to be blessed with the gift of prophecy in the Bible. We are told of another, later prophetess, one Hulda, who lived in the days of King Josiah. Hulda must have exerted great influence on the people. For the king after the discovery by the high priest Hilkiah of "the book of the law in the house of the Lord," sent Hilkiah to "Hulda the prophetess, the wife of Shallum, the son of Harhas, keeper of the wardrobe," to "inquire of the Lord for me, and for the people, and for all Judah, concerning the words of this book that is found; for great is the wrath of the Lord that is kindled against us, because our fathers have not hearkened unto the words of this book, to do according unto all that which is written concerning us." Modern scholars believe that the "Book of the Law" that was found "in the house of the Lord" was Deuteronomy.

Post-biblical tradition also endows Sarah the wife of Abraham, Abigail the wife of David, Hannah the mother of the prophet Samuel, and even Esther, cousin of Mordecai, with the prophetic gift. Other women were credited with saving cities from destruction and counseling kings.

Woman in Talmudic Times

Like the Bible, the Talmud is full of many statements testifying to the merit, piety, steadfastness, and moral calibre of women. Thus, the Talmud at one point declares that the children of Israel were liberated from bondage in Egypt for the sake of the saintly women amongst them. Elsewhere, it goes on to assert the general rule that whenever a people is saved from oppression it is for the sake of the pious women living in their midst at the time. There were two occasions during the wanderings of the children of Israel through the desert of Sinai that the women remained steadfast to their faith and national destiny in the face of popular clamor. The first came when the children of Israel pressed Aaron to make them a Golden Calf that they might worship. According to the Midrash, Aaron tried to delay matters by asking for contributions of gold and silver with which to make the calf. The men responded enthusiastically, but the women refused to give up their rings and bracelets for so sacrilegious a purpose, saying, "How dare we anger God, who has brought great miracles to pass in our behalf, redeeming us from Egypt, and allowing us to cross the Red Sea unharmed?"

The second instance of feminine intrepidity occurred after the spies whom Moses had sent to Canaan to "spy out the land" came back with an unfavorable report. The men raised the cry, "Let us make a captain and let us return to Egypt." But the women, discounting the exaggerated account of the fearfulness of the inhabitants of the Promised Land, would not agree. They insisted on going forward to conquer Canaan, in accordance with the will of God.

Then, again, the Talmud frequently refers to the more "womanly" qualities. Woman is by nature tender-hearted, more "understanding" than man. "Understanding," of course, refers to woman's intuition—the native insight that enables the gentler sex to form a more accurate estimate of the true character of persons. Hence, "A woman watches a guest more narrowly than a man." More modest than a man, a woman is more easily and profoundly shamed. The sages assumed that a woman would be hesitant to bring suit in court, preferring to suffer rather than undergo the embarrassment of publicly arguing her case. On this assumption, Jewish law gives women's cases precedence on the calendar; if a number of cases are on the docket, one involving a woman litigant is dealt with first.

"And Ruth said, entreat me not to leave thee, and to return from following after thee; for whither thou goest, I will go; and where thou lodgest I will lodge: thy people shall be my people, and thy God my God." . . . Ruth 1:16

It is true, inevitably, the Talmud does contain a number of uncomplimentary remarks about so-called feminine characteristics: overcuriosity, talkativeness, frivolity, fickleness, and other faults that men have always attributed to women, in every age and nation. Nevertheless, despite the witty or sarcastic remarks at their expense, the sex emerges with a favorable balance in Talmudic and post-Talmudic literature. Women are more to be praised than dispraised. Certainly, in religious terms, "Women are more prompt than men in fulfilling the commandments."

This is not to imply that our forefathers were blind to the obvious physical charms of womankind. All the heroines in the Bible and Talmud are appreciated for their beauty. Sarah, as we have mentioned, was "a very fair woman," Rebecca "a damsel very fair to look upon." So was Zipporah, Moses' wife. The classic hymn to feminine beauty, of course, is the Song of Songs, where the lover describes the charms of his beloved.

So it is not that Judaism lacks appreciation of physical beauty. Rather, our religion holds that beauty of character is more important. The thirty-first chapter of the Book of Proverbs is a description of the ideal woman, "whose price is far above rubies." The "woman of valor" is a good business woman and a good worker. But perhaps her chief virtue is her charity: "She stretcheth forth her hand to the poor, yea, she reacheth forth her hand to the needy." The poet concludes: "Many daughters have done valiantly, but thou excellest them all." What does her excellence consist of? Beauty? Charm? Neither. "For grace is deceitful, and beauty is vain, but a woman that feareth the Lord, she shall be praised." Fear of God in the Bible always carries a connotation of awe and reverence, an attitude of obedience to the will of God which is the ground of Jewish morality, as well as of religious piety.

To sum up the Jewish traditional attitude toward women: A woman may attain excellence even without physical beauty if she is endowed with moral beauty— that is, has a good character. For mere physical beauty may at times lead merely to vanity, while moral beauty is necessary for a woman to be able to fulfill the important functions of her life—as wife, and as mother.

"Then said Boaz unto Ruth: 'Hearest thou not, my daughter? Go not to glean
in another field, neither pass from hence, but abide here fast by my maidens' " . . .
Ruth 2:8

MICHAL, SAUL'S DAUGHTER, as played by Sara Feinstein for Habima Haketana, New York

"You descend ever farther, ever deeper, engulfed in a haze, and
     vanish from my eyes.
Alas, my beloved, why have you forsaken me?
For whom shall I cherish my charms, my beauty?
Who shall delight in my youth and my grace?
Cursed be my beauty if David reject it!"
(From drama by A. Ashman)

Education and Religious Participation

It is undeniable that there was a period during the recent past when pious Jews, especially those living in the smaller towns of Eastern Europe, neglected the Jewish education of their daughters. They justified this omission by quoting a statement from the Talmud made by Rabbi Eliezer of the third century: "He who teaches his daughter Torah is teaching her a subject for which she has neither taste nor inclination." But Rabbi Eliezer was contradicted by a contemporary rabbi, Bar Azzai, who declared: "A father is obliged to teach his daughter the Torah." It was Bar Azzai's view that prevailed—in fact, Rabbi Eliezer did not practice what he preached. He himself married a wife famous for her learning—there are many instances of her intelligence and knowledge cited in the Talmud.

Throughout the ages, Jewish communities all over the world have made strong efforts to provide girls with a proper Jewish education. There are numerous statements in our early rabbinic writings urging that the girls be educated. And then we have many accounts of how such education was organized and conducted. From one passage in the Mishnah we gather that it was customary for the Palestinian Jews to

24

teach their daughters the Bible. From another Mishnah we learn that women had sufficient education to qualify as teachers.

We have evidence that later, during the early Middle Ages in Babylonia, the Jews did not neglect their daughters' education. Rab Hai, who lived in the tenth and eleventh centuries, wrote a poem that contained the lines: "If sons and daughters be born to you, be mild in your discipline; spare neither effort nor money, and buy them books for their studies. Above all, engage a teacher for them from their early youth." And Rabbi Petahyah of Regensburg, who visited the Near East during the years 1175-1185, tells us about the distinguished daughter of the Gaon, or leader of the community, Samuel Ha-Levi. She was so well versed in the Talmud that she lectured to the students of her father's academy.

The same was true in Germany during the Middle Ages. A famous scholar, Eliezer the son of Samuel Ha-Levi, who lived in Mayence in the twelfth and thirteenth centuries, wrote in the testament he left his children: "My sons and daughters, endeavor by all means to dwell in a large Jewish community, so that your sons and daughters may receive instruction in Torah." And Judah Hasid (the Pious) of Regensburg, who died in 1217, author of the famous *Book of the Pious,* said: "One is obligated to teach one's daughter Hebrew, so that she may know how to pray. One must also teach her the important laws regulating the observance of the ritual commandments."

HAMAN PLEADS FOR HIS LIFE WITH ESTHER
(Edward Armitage, 1817-96)

In fact, the Jews of Germany were so zealous in educating their daughters that they earned the admiring envy of their Christian neighbors. The famous scholastic theologian, Peter Abelard, who lived in the eleventh and twelfth centuries, wrote:

Christians who dedicate a son to the priesthood do so principally for gain. They know that a priest leaves no heirs, so all his property reverts to his family. Not so with the Jews. Their zeal for their God and their love of His Torah lead them to send all their children to school, that they may be versed in the Torah. Even the poorest father, with as many as ten children, will send his daughters as well as his sons to be trained in the Torah and Jewish lore.

Nor were the Jewries of Eastern Europe behind their Central European brethren in this respect. Judah the Pious, whom we have mentioned above, tells us that travelers who had visited the Jewish communities in the Slavonic countries (Bohemia, Poland, Lithuania) reported that there were many women in those countries who were able to recite by heart whole chapters from the Book of Isaiah. We also have first-hand records. Documents treating of community organization in various Polish cities during this age tell us that a number of Jewish communities maintained separate schools for girls. Other historical records report that the general rule was for girls to be given private instruction at home by tutors.

Even in Jewish communities in the Far East, in India, for example, there were families that took special pains for the education of their daughters. Professor Simha Assaf, author of a history of Jewish education, writes that there were Indian Jewish women who were remarkable for their mastery of the Bible in the original Hebrew, as well as for their attainments in the Mishnah and Aggada. (Jews emigrated to India from the Iraqi communities of Bagdad, Mosul, and Basra during the nineteenth century.) These learned women were able to test the scholarship of representatives of charitable institutions in Jerusalem who visited India to raise funds.

JEWISH GIRLS — BOMBAY, INDIA
(courtesy, Hazel Greenwald, New York)

DAYDREAMING — A JEWESS
sculpture by Rosa Newman-Walinska

Thus, Jews all over the world have always seen to the education of their daughters, as well as their sons. Besides, the very home atmosphere encouraged the knowledge of a minimum of information about the Jewish religion and its observances. There was an attitude of love, devotion, and reverence for traditional learning. The home atmosphere was full of loyalty to the Jewish tradition. The parents always were "talking Torah." The father's conversation was usually seasoned with Biblical proverbs, Talmudic quotations, stories, and legends. And then, during the period from the sixteenth to the nineteenth century, a body of extensive religious and moral literature in medieval and modern Yiddish developed that was intended especially for girls and women, and which they read and studied. These books were translations and comments on the Bible, together with quotations and legends from all of Jewish literature. Here is an example from the very popular *Tze-ena U-reena* published in 1590:

"And the Lord God caused a deep sleep to fall upon Adam, and he slept: and He took one of his ribs, and closed up the flesh instead thereof.

"And the rib which the Lord God had taken from man made he a woman, and brought her unto the man." (Genesis 3:21-22).

27

This is to teach us that a man should not storm against his wife at times when he sees a thing that does not please him. He must act as though he is asleep and does not see. And when God brought all the creatures before the First Man to give them names, Adam saw every animal and every beast had a wife. So Adam said, All the creatures have wives, and I have none. That is why God caused a deep sleep to fall upon Adam and took one of his ribs and made him a woman. God made Adam sleep so that the woman would not be hateful unto him seeing that she had come out of his own body. And when a person is deserving God sends him a wife to love him and to be a helpmeet unto him. But if a person is not pious, God sends him a wife as hateful to him as his body, who makes him to lose his share in this world, and in the hereafter, too. She is worse than death. Also, a good wife brings her man his share in the hereafter, as we find from the story of one pious man. He had a wife who was an exceedingly pious woman. But they had no children, so he gave her a writ of divorcement. She took a husband who was dreadfully wicked and turned him into a pious man—and he took a dreadfully wicked woman to wife and became wicked himself.

There were also widely read codes of conduct and selections from morality books written in Yiddish, intended to guide the reader along the path of charity and kindness. And, finally, perhaps most effective, were the many stories and poems imbued with the best spirit of Judaism. All these influences combined to prepare Jewish girls for their place in Jewish society: as mother and wife, to share in the perpetuation of Jewish values and to help mold the character of the next generation.

Women in Jewish Law

On the whole, women are under a slight disability when it comes to observing Jewish laws. The general rule is that women, like men, are obligated to observe all prohibitions, all "Thou shalt not's." The case is somewhat different in respect to affirmative precepts, or "Thou shalt's." They are not required to observe affirmative precepts that fall due at a definite time. For example, phylacteries are put on only at the time of prayer—so women need not put them on. Then, again, the *shofar*, or ram's horn, is blown only on the High Holy Days, so women need not participate in the blowing ceremony. There is a seven-day limit to eating in the Succah during the Feast of Tabernacles, or Succoth—so women need not eat there.

There are, however, exceptions to this general rule. Traditionally, women are obligated to eat a certain amount of matzoth on the first night of Passover (the formula is "an amount the size of an olive"), despite the fact that there is a time limit on Passover. Like men, too, women must recite the regular prayers (except for the Shema), and say grace. There are also two precepts that the rabbis prescribed for women: they must share in the lighting of the Hannukah candles, and listen to, or themselves read from, the Purim Megillah, or Scroll. In fact, a woman may read the Megillah to a group of men, who, by their active listening, are performing the Purim Megillah precept themselves.

What is not generally understood is that women who wish to observe the precepts that are limited as to time, though they are not under any obligation to do so, are fully *permitted* to observe them if they wish. Some of the precepts have always been observed by women—for example, all Jews, regardless of sex, have always listened to the blowing of the shofar on the High Holy Days.

Why were women released from the obligation of performing the time-limited precepts? The Talmud attempts to base this practice on an interpretation of several Biblical verses. Later scholars believed the original limitation arose because it was thought that women might find it impossible to perform certain of the precepts, particularly those with a time limit attached to them, because of the pressure of bringing up children. So they were allowed to forgo those precepts.

Marriage

The institution of marriage is regarded by Judaism as one of the utmost sacredness and the highest value. In fact, the term for the ceremony of the marriage union is called *Kiddushin*, literally meaning "act of consecration." The view is that the two persons about to be married are consecrating themselves to one another.

REMBRANDT'S "THE GREAT JEWISH BRIDE"
(British Museum)

The Bible describes God as creating woman for the very purpose of marriage. "And the Lord God said, It is not good that the man should be alone; I will make him an help meet for him." Elsewhere, the Bible declares, "Whoso findeth a wife findeth a good thing, and obtaineth favor of the Lord."

The Talmud goes still further, asserting that an unmarried person is not entitled to be known as Adam, or a human being. "For it is written, 'Male and female created he them; and blessed them and called their name Adam' "—only when man and woman are united, are they entitled to the blessing and the name of human being. Another Talmudic passage declares: "He who has no wife lacks joy, blessing, and even life itself, for life without those things is not really life." One of the sages attributed the death of Nadab and Abihu, the sons of Aaron, to the fact that they were not married. Aaron's sons were killed when they entered the Tabernacle to burn incense; had they been married, their value would have been enhanced, and they would have been worthy to offer the incense in that holiest of places.

In view of their high opinion of marriage, it is not to be wondered at that the ancient sages regarded marriage as a good in itself, and frowned on marriages of convenience for any ulterior purpose. They were particularly severe against marriage for money, insisting that money won through marriage would bring no blessing and would speedily be lost. On the other hand, "Happy is the man whose wife is both beautiful and of good character, for he will live long."

On the whole, though, a good character was considered more important in a wife than beauty. Joshua ben Sira, who lived about the year 200 C.E. and wrote a Book of Proverbs that was not included in the Bible, said: "A good wife is a good present and a gift of God." When asked "Who can be considered rich?" a sage mentioned in the Talmud replied, "He whose wife is distinguished for her good deeds." Another sage interpreted the verse in Proverbs, "He that is of a merry heart hath a continual feast" as referring to the man who has a good wife, "for she labors to bring him joy and remove all anguish." Conversely, the woman of bad character is deadly. The author of Ecclesiastes declares: "And I find more bitter than death the woman, whose heart is snares and nets, and her hands as bands; whoso pleaseth God shall escape from her; but the sinner shall be taken by her." And the Talmud avers: "All evil is sufferable, except an evil wife."

Age of Marriage

In Jewish law, a girl stops being a minor child and becomes an adult at the age of twelve; a boy becomes an adult at the age of thirteen. But the girl does not attain her full majority at once. There is a period of transition that lasts for six months and a day. During that time the girl is known as a *Naarah* ("young woman"); at the end of this period, she is called a *Bogeret* ("mature woman").

A boy who is still a minor cannot become engaged or marry on his own

THE WEDDING CANOPY
by Maurycy Gottlieb, 1856-79

31

initiative. After thirteen, he can, although the Mishnah considers eighteen to be the proper age for a man to marry. So long as she is a minor or a Naarah, a woman is under her father's authority in respect to marriage; only her father has the right to give her in marriage—with her consent, of course. If a woman takes the initiative herself, and marries without her father's consent, in Jewish traditional law the marriage is invalid. The exception is in the case of an orphan. The minor can be given in marriage by her mother and brothers. The young woman who is an orphan immediately attains her majority and has full right to marry on her own initiative.

However, Jewish authorities have always looked with disfavor on the marriage of minors, though legally they are permissible. No less an authority than Rab, the leading Babylonian scholar, said: "It is prohibited for a father to marry off a minor daughter before she grows up and is able to choose her own husband." This view is recorded in the most authoritative code of Jewish laws and customs, the Shulhan Aruk of Joseph Karo. Unfortunately, this rule was not always followed. In many countries during the Middle Ages, and in the Russian Empire as late as the early nineteenth century, there were frequent cases of marrying off minors. However, there were extenuating circumstances (such as avoidance of harsh and discriminatory military service), and Jewish authorities continually apologized for the practice.

Judaism has always regarded marriage as a communal concern; Jewish communities made every effort to help poor or orphaned girls to get married. Almost every Jewish community had a special Haknasat Kalaah society that tried to arrange suitable matches and supply needy unmarried girls with dowries. The sages considered this a valuable kind of social service—it was a mitzvah, or religious act of virtue, that was bound to be rewarded, in the Hereafter if not on earth. Many tales are told in the Talmud and later Jewish literature about pious folk who gave all their possessions to help poor girls find good husbands. One such story deals with Rabbi Eliezer, who lived in the first half of the second century. Rabbi Eliezer had gone to market to purchase the clothing and other things he needed for his daughter's marriage. At the market place he met community officials trying to raise funds to marry off two orphans. "These orphans come before my own daughter," Rabbi Eliezer cried, giving the officials all the money he had in his pocket.

Nathan Hanover, the chronicler of Jewish persecution in Poland and Lithuania during the Chmelnitzki uprising of 1648-49, tells us that no poor girl over eighteen was allowed to continue unmarried in those countries. The pious women in those Eastern European communities left no stone unturned to marry off the needy and orphaned.

Marriage Ceremony

Practically up to the tenth century, there were two steps in marriage. The first was the betrothal *(Erusin)*, where the groom performed the act of Kiddushin in the presence of witnesses. This ceremony, in which the groom recited the formula of

KETUBAH — a marriage contract listing the details of the marriage agreement.

sanctification, gave the bride the status of a married woman, but with certain limitations. Bride and groom did not live together, the bride remaining in her father's house for a period of time—a year at the most. Nor was the groom under the obligation of supporting his betrothed during this period.

The second step, called *Nesuin,* was the marriage ceremony proper. Completing the marriage, the bride and groom stood under a canopy *(Huppah)* and signed the marriage contract *(Ketubah),* reciting the appropriate benediction. From that time forward, they lived together as man and wife, in the full sense. After the tenth century, however, both Erusin and Nesuin, betrothal and marriage, were combined in one ceremony.

According to Talmudic law, the groom can perform the act of Kiddushin by giving the bride a coin of a specified value, or any article or object (including food) to the same value, as he pronounces the betrothal formula ("Be thou betrothed to me according to the law of Moses and Israel") in the presence of witnesses. However, around the seventh century it became customary in Palestine for the groom to perform the Kiddushin by placing a gold or silver ring on the finger of his betrothed. Soon the custom spread to Babylonia, Persia, and other Oriental countries. For a time it was customary in Babylonia for the groom to present the bride with a cup of wine containing the ring, saying, "Be thou sanctified to me by the cup of wine and what it contains." Soon the practice of sanctification by the ring spread to all European countries.

The reading and writing of the Ketubah constitute an important part of the marriage ceremony. The Ketubah states the duties that the husband assumes toward his wife—namely, to support her, clothe her, and to pay her, if they should be divorced (through his estate, if he should die) an additional sum; if the wife brings a dowry, the husband guarantees to repay her, in the event of divorce or death. The sum fixed by law varies according to the wife's status: if she has never been married before, she receives the full amount, if she has been a widow or a divorcee half the amount.

In earlier times, the wife could insist on a clause in the Ketubah stipulating that her male children should inherit the Ketubah money if she were to die before her husband. Later, this condition was abolished.

There were other conditions frequently stipulated in the Ketubah. In countries where polygamy was practiced, there might be a stipulation in the Ketubah to the effect that the husband could not take a second wife without the first wife's consent. In some places, a clause in the Ketubah spared the wife the necessity of appealing to her husband's kin to marry her, or to give up the claim to marriage, in the event of her husband's death. (This practice was known as *Halitzah.*) An ingenious clause in the Ketubah stated that the husband assumed the obligation to write a conditional divorce if he became dangerously sick. This divorce would become valid only on his death—and so his widow, having been divorced from him, would not have to appeal to his kinsmen for Halitzah. If the husband did not die, the conditional divorce would not be in force.

Although the Bible does not prohibit polygamy (like most Oriental kings, David and Solomon had many wives), monogamy was always considered the ideal state of marriage. This is evident from the literary symbolism that the prophets used— they compared God's relations with Israel to the relations between husband and wife in a good marriage. Soon after the Kingdom of Judah was broken up and its inhabitants sent into Babylonian exile in 586 B.C.E., monogamy became the rule, polygamy the exception. Thus, the prophet Malachi inveighed against those who took a second wife: "The Lord hath been witness between thee and the wife of thy youth, against whom thou hast dealt treacherously; yet is she thy companion and the wife of thy covenant." Apparently, monogamy was the general practice, and polygamists were regarded, as Malachi indicates, as sacrilegious.

There is not a single reference in the literature produced during the Second Commonwealth to indicate that any of the Hasmonean princes practiced polygamy. True, Herod had nine wives; the very fact that the historian Josephus felt it necessary to apologize for Herod (the excuse was that polygamy was legal) leads us to conclude that it was not common. (Nor was Herod in any way an ideal Jewish king!) The same situation continued during the days of the Talmud and after: monogamy was the rule. Not a single one of the masters and geonim had more than one wife. In later times, particularly in the Orient under the influence of Islam, and to some extent in Europe too, Jews did have more than one wife. Finally, Rabbi Gershon, known in Jewish tradition as the "Light of the Exile," who lived in the tenth and eleventh centuries, decreed that polygamy be punished by extreme excommunication; at once accepted, this decree acquired the sanction of law among all of European Jewry. At the present time, the State of Israel punishes polygamy severely by law.

Relations between Husband and Wife

The wife has a highly respected place in the Jewish family. This despite the fact that traditional Jewish law places a number of restrictions on the rights of the married woman—her husband has the right to profit from her labor and enjoy the income (not the capital) of her private property. But time and again, Jewish literature emphasizes the husband's obligation to honor his wife and treat her with the greatest possible consideration. The Talmud says: "The verse in Job reading, 'And thou shalt know that thy tabernacle shall be in peace; and thou shalt visit thy habitation, and shalt not sin'—refers to the husband who loves his wife as himself and honors her even more than he would desire to be honored by others." Another passage in the Talmud advises: "A man should spend less than he can afford on his own clothing, as much as he can afford on his children's clothing, and more than he can afford on his wife's clothing." A leading Talmudic master urged husbands to treat their wives with particular respect because, said he, "The only reason a home is blessed is because of the wife."

The same theme recurs in later literature, particularly in the numerous testaments left by eminent individuals. Maimonides tells his children in his last testament, "Honor your wives, for they constitute your honor." Abraham Hurwitz, a leading sixteenth-century scholar, urges his sons to preserve a loving relationship with their wives at all costs. Hurwitz reminds his sons that the Talmud advises husbands never to quarrel with their wives, even when provoked by their ill temper. Rather, the husband ought to endeavor to understand the cause of his wife's disturbance, and speak to her soothingly.

According to Jewish law, neither death nor divorce ought to affect the warm relations between husband and wife. The husband is obligated to arrange a funeral for his wife that is appropriate to her status and worth, and to place a tombstone on her grave. The *Book of the Pious,* to which we have referred earlier, advises a husband not to remarry until his dead wife's friends have ceased talking about her and expressing their sorrow at her loss. Leading rabbinical authorities would have the widower wait until after the three chief holidays have passed—for at these times his loss of his wife would have most deeply impressed itself on his memory.

Remarkably enough, in Jewish tradition the husband is expected to help his divorced wife if she is in need, even if she has remarried. There are numerous

"I FOUND MY LOVE"
by Chaim Gross

35

accounts in the Talmud of scholars aiding divorced wives—even to the extent of supporting both their former wives and their second husbands.

Divorce

On the whole, the Jewish attitude toward divorce is a liberal one. The School of Hillel held that there were other justifications for divorce beside adultery and irreligious behavior; general incompatibility, as well as domestic mismanagement, were also in their opinion grounds for divorce. Rabbi Akiba went still further: he permitted divorce in cases where there had simply been a change for the worse in the husband's attitude toward his wife. The School of Hillel's view is now the accepted one. However, Judaism generally regards divorce with disfavor, particularly in the case of a first marriage. The Talmudic sages comment, in their usual picturesque style, "Even the altar weeps when a man divorces his first wife."

In Jewish law, the husband is the only one with the right to sue for divorce. The court has no right to grant a divorce, nor can a wife, except in certain cases to be mentioned below, sue for one. Originally, Talmudic law permitted a husband to divorce his wife even against her will. But from the tenth century on, after the "Decree of Rabbi Gershom" *(see above)*, the principle has been established that no man can divorce his wife without her consent. This has been the guiding principle of Jewish law for the past thousand years. Divorce is valid only by mutual agreement.

There are certain circumstances under which either husband or wife can ask the court to issue an enforced divorce: for example, when the husband is suffering from an incurable or dangerous disease or engaged in a disagreeable occupation, or when the wife behaves improperly in terms of Jewish religious law. Under such circumstances, the court forces the offending party to agree to a divorce. The wife, when adjudged the guilty party, forfeits the Ketubah money stipulated as due her at divorce.

The bill of divorcement is written and issued by the court; the court further sees to it that all the regulations for the writing of a bill of divorcement are met. The husband need not hand the bill directly to his wife; it can be transmitted through an agent. The execution of a divorce is extremely complicated; so it is carried out before a court of three, including at least one rabbi versed in the various rules and regulations governing divorce.

Traditionally, Jewish law would not accept civil divorce in lieu of the stringent forms that characterized Jewish divorce. It is current practice, however, not to issue a Jewish divorce unless it has been preceded by civil divorce.

According to Biblical law, a man who is not a priest (a Cohen) may remarry his divorced wife, unless she has been remarried in the interim.

Widows and Orphans

Widows and orphans, particularly when the latter are young girls, are treated with extraordinary care under Jewish law. The Bible emphasizes a number of times that these unfortunates are entitled to special consideration. "Ye shall not afflict any widow, or fatherless child. If thou afflict them in any wise, and they cry at all unto me, I will surely hear their cry; and my wrath shall wax hot . . ." God is said "to execute justice for the fatherless and the widows." The widowed are not to be taken advantage of economically: the Bible's warning "Thou shalt not take the widow's raiment as a pledge" is interpreted by the Mishnah to apply to the rich widow as well as to the poor. Jewish law insists that if a husband stipulates in his will that his widow is to receive no income from his estate, this stipulation is to be ignored.

The orphaned girl has certain advantages in Jewish law. If the estate left by her father is not large enough to maintain both the son and the daughter, the daughter has the prior claim—the son may even have to go begging. Likewise, if there are two orphans, one a boy and one a girl, and both are in need of support from charity, the girl has the prior claim. The same is true when the need is for assistance in marriage. The general rule in traditional Jewish law and ethics was to favor the woman because her sex placed her in a less favorable position in ancient society.

Role as Mother

When Deborah, proud of her success as the leader of her people in battle, sang a song of victory, she could think of no higher title to give herself than "a mother in Israel." "The inhabitants of the villages ceased, they ceased in Israel, until that I Deborah arose, that I arose a mother in Israel." Throughout Jewish history, the appellation of "mother" was the greatest mark of honor for a woman. In fact, the same term is used in the Bible to designate the nation as a whole, to which every individual Jew owes love, honor, and loyalty. Thus, the prophet Isaiah, wishing to emphasize that the Jews were suffering as a punishment for their individual sins, not because God had broken his covenant with His chosen people, cries out: "Where is the bill of your mother's divorcement whom I have put away?"

The Bible and Talmud are full of passages stressing the importance of the mother's role in molding her children's character, and that of the nation as a whole. The Book of Proverbs, for example, frequently stresses the value of a mother's instruction: "My son, hear the instruction of thy father, and forsake not the law of thy mother"; "My son, keep thy father's commandment, and forsake not the law of thy mother."

The mother in Jewish tradition is regarded as laying the foundation of the children's character, on which the father later builds. Thus, the Mekilta, one of the oldest books of morality of the Midrash, asserts that Moses told the women about the Torah before he told the men. The ancient sages explain that in the verse, "Thus shalt thou say to the House of Jacob, and tell the children of Israel," the "House of Jacob" refers to the women, who are the foundation of the home. A medieval moralist adds that the reason why women are conceded precedence in the establishment of a home is that it is they who bring up the children, send them off to school, and influence them to virtue. According to Jewish law, in mixed marriages involving Jews and non-Jews the child's identification depends on that of the mother: if the mother is Jewish, the child is Jewish; the child is non-Jewish if the mother is non-Jewish. This is apparently another recognition of the paramount influence of the mother on the child's personality.

Of course, we are all familiar with the Fifth Commandment which tells us, "Honor thy father and thy mother." It is repeated elsewhere in the Bible in a slightly altered form: "Ye shall fear every man his mother and his father." (Fear cannot be commanded; what is meant is an attitude of respectful reverence.) Incidentally, the Talmudic sages have an ingenious explanation of why the Bible tells us to honor first our father and then our mother, but to fear first our mother and then our father. God, they say, knows that a child usually honors his mother more than his father, for she is more kindly to him, attending to his personal needs. So God tells us to honor our fathers more than we are apt to. On the other hand, the child is likely to respect his father more than he does his mother, since his father teaches him the Torah—so God tells us to treat our mothers with greater reverence than is our natural wont.

There are a number of anecdotes in Jewish literature illustrating the remarkable lengths great scholars and leaders went to in honoring their mothers. One such anecdote, involving Rabbi Tarphon, is characteristic. It seems that one day Rabbi Tarphon's mother was walking in her garden on the Sabbath when her shoelace tore and the shoe fell off her foot. It being the Sabbath, repairing it was not permissible. Tarphon, to spare his mother the pain of walking barefoot on the pebbled ground, laid his hand under her foot for her to walk on. The same rabbi was in the habit of offering his mother his back on which to step when ascending or descending her high bed. Once his mother complained to a number of visiting scholars that her son gave her too much honor. They replied that her son could never honor her sufficiently, though he offered her twice, or three times the respect he did.

Women of Distinction

Queen Salome Alexandra, wife of Aleander Jannaeus, reigned for nine years (76-65 Before the Common Era), and her reign was distinguished by peace, prosperity, and learning.

Beruria, wife of the Talmudic master Rabbi Meir, was famed for her learning and piety. She took part in complicated legal discussions, and statements of hers are incorporated in the Mishnah, as are ethical mottoes that she composed.

There is a famous story illustrating Beruria's remarkable fortitude and religious sentiment. It happened that two of her children died on a Sabbath, while her husband, Rabbi Meir, was lecturing at the academy. Beruria laid the dead children in bed, and covered the bodies with a sheet. When her husband came home that evening and asked for the children, Beruria answered that they had gone to the Academy. She waited until Rabbi Meir had performed the Havdalah ceremony, signifying the

A JEWISH MOTHER by Anna Walinska

end of the Sabbath. When he had finished, Beruria said: "Meir, I have a question to ask you. This morning, a man gave me a valuable pledge to hold for him; now he asks it back. Shall I return it?"

"Of course," said Rabbi Meir. "You must return a pledge."

Beruria then took her husband to the bedroom and showed him his dead children. He began to cry.

"Did you not tell me," said Beruria, "that one must return a pledge? God took back the precious jewels that he left with us as a pledge."

Rachel, daughter of Rashi, the most famous commentator on the Bible and Talmud, used to write legal decisions for her father when he was too weak to write them himself. We have Rashi's own testimony to that effect.

Jacob Mölim, the great authority on synagogue ritual and custom, who lived in the fourteenth and fifteenth centuries, quotes in his Responsa to legal questions the views of his two sisters, Bonlin and Simhah.

In the time of the Muslim prophet Mohammed, during the first half of the seventh century, there was a woman known by the name of Sarah who was famous as a poet. One of her poems has been preserved: it is an elegy on the death of a leader of the Bnai Kuraizo, a Jewish tribe, who was murdered by Mohammed. She was said to have carried on guerrilla warfare against the prophet of Islam herself, and to have been murdered by a Muslim agent.

The daughter of the famous poet Judah ha-Levi wrote a number of Hebrew poems, one of which is included among her father's collected works.

Rebecca, daughter of the great scholar Rabbi Meir Tiktiner who died in 1550, composed a Yiddish book called *Meneket Rivkah*. It contains moral teachings, selections from the Talmud, Midrash, and other ethical books, as well as several poems in Hebrew and Yiddish. Rebecca also translated the famous ethical treatise by Bahya ibn Pakuda from Hebrew into Yiddish.

Sara Kafia Sulam, who died in 1651, was a distinguished Venetian linguist, with a mastery of Hebrew, Latin, and Spanish, as well as her native Italian. Versed in philosophy, she composed an essay on the Jewish conception of immortality. Sulam also wrote Italian poetry.

A woman known only as Sarah the daughter of Mordecai wrote a large number of Yiddish religious poems for all occasions under the pen name of Sarah Bath Tobim ("the daughter of the pious"). Typically feminine, they were popular for centuries as *Techinot*. During the nineteenth century, a number of men assumed the same pseudonym to write similar Yiddish prayers.

Rachel Morporgo of Padua (1790-1871) was a granddaughter of the famous Hebrew poet Moses Hayyim Luzzatto. She achieved recognition in her own right for her learning in Talmud and Jewish philosophy and distinction as a Hebrew poet. In 1890, the centennial of her birth, a volume of her poems was published. They were translated into German by Ludwig August Frankel.

During modern times hundreds of Jewesses, whose names are generally known have distinguished themselves in such widely divergent fields as the stage, the bench, the laboratory, politics, music and art, medicine, literature, social work, and pure scholarship.

GLUECKEL VON HAMELN
1646 - 1724

Jewish life in Germany during the latter half of the seventeenth century was most difficult. But to the shrewd eyes of Glueckel, whose MEMOIRS have been translated into many languages, there was much to be seen that was warm and gay.

Glueckel was born in Hamburg in 1646, the daughter of Loeb Pinkerle, a jewel dealer. Three years later the Jews were expelled from Hamburg, not to return until 1657.

Glueckel was only fourteen when she married Chayim Hameln. During the thirty years of their marriage, which she described as the "happiest in all the world," she bore fourteen children. When Chayim died in 1689, Glueckel successfully took over his business affairs. All her children married well, and became outstanding members of their communities.

Glueckel received a fair education. Her MEMOIRS show familiarity with the Bible, prayerbook, and many of the secular books available to her.

In 1700 Glueckel married the well-known banker Cerf Levy. Within a few years, having lost his own fortune as well as hers, he passed away. Glueckel spent the rest of her life with her children.

Acclaimed the greatest actress of her day, Rachel was the daughter of a poor Swiss peddler. Born in Mumpf, Switzerland, in 1820, she was named Elisa Rachel Felix. To augment the family income she and a sister sang in the cafes of Lyons and Paris while still children.

There they attracted the attention of a famous singer, who helped train them for careers on the stage. When only seventeen, Rachel appeared at the Comédie Francaise in the role of Camille, and at once attained stardom. Wherever she appeared in London, Brussels, Berlin, Leningrad, and the United States (which she toured in 1855), Rachel was greeted with fiery enthusiasm.

She played the leading roles in many dramas by Racine, Corneille, and Voltaire. A number of plays were written especially for her.

In 1858, only 37 years old, Rachel died in Cannes, France. Her beauty and talent, so highly acclaimed in her own day, have remained a legend among lovers of the theater.

RACHEL
1820 - 1858

Sara Bernhardt was of Dutch-Jewish descent, and she became "the golden voice" of France. The greatest actress not only in France but in the world at that time, she was admired and honored by all, and worshipped by her "fans," who were by no means limited to teen-agers. Grown people kneeled and kissed her garment's hem; royal ladies laid their bouquets at her feet; kings kissed her hand. In the midst of anti-Semitic outbursts in Tsarist Russia, the aristocrats united to give her a magnificent coat and muff of specially-picked sables. So frantic were some of the tributes paid her, that Sara Bernhardt once remarked casually to a friend, "Yes, I attract all the lunatics of the world!" Actually she attracted everybody, of every age, race, and type, who saw her perform and heard her marvelous voice.

Though a passionate French patriot, she never permitted an anti-Semitic remark to pass unchallenged; she would always retort, proudly, "I, too, am a daughter of the great Jewish people!"

Described when young as a "frail little girl with great almond-shaped eyes and a rebellious mass of wavy chestnut hair," Sara Bernhardt grew into a fascinating beauty and a peerless actress. She was generous and kind, devoted to her family, always loyal to her country and to her co-religionists. When she toured in America, her success was as great as in Europe.

SARA BERNHARDT
1844-1923

41

There has never been a time when Jewish women did not attain distinction outside the home. Even in Talmudic times there were women whose learning was recognized and praised by their male colleagues. In America, Jewish women have organized great movements in support of education, and charity institutions to provide aid to the Jews of Israel and other lands. They have achieved fame in literature, art, the drama, and science. The American Jewish Community would be poor indeed without the remarkable contributions to its life and progress provided by its feminine members.

Herein are presented brief biographies of distinguished Jewesses of this country and Europe—a mere sampling of the vast range of women's achievements in Judaism and the world.

PENINA MOISE
1797-1880

A poor, small home in Charleston, South Carolina, a thin old lady who had been blind for twenty-five years—and yet, when Penina Moise died and that home was empty, young people and children who had known her wept for an irreplaceable friend, and Jews all over the country felt that a light had gone out in Israel.

Before Penina Moise was born, in 1797, her family had been wealthy planters in the West Indies. A revolt of the slaves resulted in the massacre of many slave-owners. But the Moises had, in accordance with the Mosaic law as well as their own hearts, been humane and fair to their servants. One Negro, a leader of the revolt, aroused the family in time to escape. They fled to South Carolina with just the clothes they wore and a few valuables. The father never regained financial security. When Penina was twelve, he died.

Penina tried to help the family by making fine laces and embroidery, which she sold. The strain on her eyes weakened them, and in later life she became blind. She taught children, wrote hymns and religious poems; she counseled and helped young people. She nursed her invalid mother, and when fire and epidemic brought tragedy to Charleston, Penina Moise with endless patience and courage, nursed and fed and aided many of the victims. The fame of her radiant personality as well as her verses brought constant visitors to her home, making it a literary salon as well as a place for spiritual help and comfort.

How many millions of people from many nations have visited the Statue of Liberty in the great New York City harbor? Just so many have seen and read at least one of the poems of the American Jewess, Emma Lazarus.

For when France in 1883 sent this enormous statue to the United States as a sign of friendship, it was necessary to raise funds to build the pedestal on the island selected for the statue site. Emma Lazarus, already known for her poetry, donated to the fund-raising auction a sonnet which she had just written on the subject of the statue. The sum of fifteen hundred dollars was offered for it (this would be about ten thousand dollars today). It was decided that the poem be engraved on the pedestal of the statue.

Emma Lazarus at first wrote poetry that dealt with the ancient Greek and Roman classics rather than with Jewish history or Jewish life. But as she grew more mature, she turned more and more to the romance and tragedy of Hebrew lore. *The Dance to Death* is one of her noted poems on Jewish legend.

EMMA LAZARUS
1849-1887

From the American city of Baltimore, to the turmoil, tragedy and danger of Palestine under the British mandate, came Henrietta Szold. Eldest and most brilliant of the eight daughters of the learned Hungarian-born Dr. Benjamin Szold, it was she who made the family name world-famous and beloved.

Before the first world war broke out in 1914, Henrietta Szold had founded the Hadassah society of women to aid the pioneers in Palestine. Beginning with thirteen young women, it has grown to nearly five hundred thousand. Without their personal aid and the large funds they have collected, the glorious story of Israel today would have been far different.

After the first world war, Henrietta Szold went to live in Palestine. Trained as a social worker, she often seemed the only one who knew how to handle the tangled individual problems of the thousands of homeless and penniless Jewish immigrants pouring into the country every day from the war-smitten lands. Living in her quiet little house in the suburbs of Jerusalem, the beauty of its flower-garden and the glories of the changing seasons across the colorful valley gave her comfort and courage for her twenty-hour workdays.

There Henrietta Szold stayed through all the difficult times, helping, serving, even raising funds and using her own money as well to care for the refugees. Henrietta Szold was one of the heroic women of America and Israel.

HENRIETTA SZOLD
1860-1945

Rebecca, daughter of the Jew, Isaac of York, is considered by many the true heroine of Sir Walter Scott's famous novel, *Ivanhoe*. Scott drew this beautiful, wise, devoted character from a living Jewess, Rebecca Gratz of Philadelphia. Scott's friend, Washington Irving, had met Rebecca Gratz; he was so struck with her beauty and sweetness that he told Scott all about her. It is possible that Scott guessed more: it may be that after the death of Irving's young fiancée (a friend of Rebecca's whom she had tenderly nursed until the end), a new love had arisen which Rebecca had rejected because she did not believe in intermarriage.

Rebecca Gratz was the seventh of twelve children born to Michael Gratz of a wealthy merchant family in Philadelphia. Hyman Gratz, her uncle, was a manager of the first Jewish Publication Society; his will established the Jewish Teachers' Training School. There was not much that a well-born girl could do in those days except volunteer social work, teaching, or nursing. Beautiful young Rebecca, besides mothering her dead sister's nine children, did all these. In 1819 she founded the Female Hebrew Benevolent Society, and served in the Philadelphia Orphans' Asylum. Her home was a gathering place for the intellectuals and artists of the time.

REBECCA GRATZ
1781-1869

LILIAN WALD
1867-1940

When Lilian Wald was a young girl, women were not expected to earn money unless they were compelled to in order to live. A sheltered daughter of wealthy German-Jewish origin, born in Cincinnati, Lilian refused to be idle. Like other good-hearted girls of her time, she became a volunteer nurse. But Lilian was no condescending "do-gooder." She visited the homes of the poor children she had nursed in the hospital. Horrified by the dirt, misery and neglect in those wretched slums, she determined to help change these conditions.

Equipped with a brilliant mind as well as a sympathetic heart, Lilian Wald helped to bring about political reforms and labor legislation; she started the Visiting Nurse Service which is still so active and helpful and now has sixteen centers. Partly as a result of her arguments and persuasions, in 1908 a Federal Charities Bureau was established by President Theodore Roosevelt.

Her great achievement was the Henry Street Settlement, where immigrant children received special education, advice, companionship; here they found greatly needed social activities, and a children's theatre which drew audiences from all New York City. Here talented youngsters found experience and gained attention; some of them later became well-known. Aline MacMahon is a famous example.

They called Lilian Wald "the Angel of Henry Street." A playground as well as a housing project in Brooklyn are named in her honor.

REBEKAH KOHUT
1864-1951

Imagine a woman so unselfish that while still young she married a much older widower with eight children and not much money. When, seven years later, her learned husband passed away, Rebekah Kohut set to work to make a living for the children. She became a social worker and teacher.

With her love and understanding of children and brilliant mind, it was natural that she should succeed. She founded the Kohut School, accommodating a hundred girls at a time. She learned the problems of young women of poor families, and worked hard to help bring about legislation to correct conditions in the factories where many of them were employed: to shorten the long working day (sometimes fourteen hours or more), to increase the miserable pay, and guarantee safety and sanitation. As head of a section of the Council of Jewish Women, Rebekah Kohut was appointed to nearly every commission in which she could serve the friendless.

LILY MONTAGU

Born to wealth and high social position, the child of an English Jewish banker who became the first Lord Swaythling, the Honorable Lily Montagu has spent her life working for the poor children and young girls of London. She established a Jewish club house where they found friendship, advice and care, and went on to decent and useful lives instead of to the jails and asylums which might have been their fate. This club soon had branches all over the world, including America.

Deeply religious, Lily Montagu was one of the first women to become a preacher in the synagogue. She was so sincere and kind in helping young delinquents, that they tried to reform themselves in order to win her praise and approval; many of them wrote her "fan letters," although she was the judge who had "sent them up"! She replied encouragingly, and rejoiced in their rehabilitation.

Lily Montagu was one of the founders and leaders of the Liberal (Reform) Jews of England. Though as a girl she had been quiet and shy, she learned to preach and speak in many countries, spreading her idea of a "living Judaism."

LADY EVA READING

The terrible crisis of the Hitler persecution proved a crucible in which were tested the souls of Jews in the safe countries. In that black year of 1933, when Hitler began his methodical destruction of six million Jews, many persons whom the world had believed to be non-Jews or indifferent to their religion came forward and declared themselves members of the Jewish faith.

Among them was Lady Eva Reading. Brought up as a Christian by her devoutly Christian mother, she had married the son of the first Lord Reading, the famous Rufus Isaacs, Chief Justice of England. But her Jewish father, Sir Alfred Mond, later made an earl with the title Lord Melchett, had educated her to a deep interest in Jewish affairs, and especially in Zionism. She and her brother had lived on his estate in Palestine, and had gained much knowledge of and sympathy with the pioneer settlers.

In the 1920's and 1930's Viscountess Erleigh (as Eva's title was then), gained distinction as a leader of Zionism; she visited Jewish communities all over the world. In 1933 she followed her father, Lord Melchett, in openly joining the Jewish community of the London Liberal Synagogue.

Lady Reading served as chairman of the Keren Hayesod in Great Britain, and as national chairman of many campaigns for the rescue and relief of the Hitler victims. In 1936 she became president of the British section of the World Jewish Congress, and was elected member of the International Executive. She is also a leading authority in England on the subject of child welfare.

BLESSED IS THE DAUGHTER

by Sulamith Ish-Kishor

You are now entering on the first steps in the life of a young woman. The world is becoming different to your eyes; people are beginning to expect of you a certain amount of responsibility. Your opinion is becoming more important; your family is beginning to be concerned about what you are going to be, rather than what you are at this moment. You are seeking new friendships, new groups. And you are beginning to dream, as all young girls do, about your chances for happiness in the occupation you may choose, and in love and marriage.

While these thoughts, these changes, these hopes and fears and wonderings, are common to all young girls at all times and in all countries, you are surely aware that for you, as a Jewish girl, there will be a few more problems. But do you know that there are also very great rewards?

You are a daughter of a people few in numbers but supremely gifted, a nation with an old and great culture on this earth, a nation that wrote one of the noblest books ever written, at the very time that its physical life was at its most primitive, that is, while it ploughed the soil with sticks, lived in tents, took pitchers to the well for water, counted its wealth in heads of cattle. From this Bible of the Hebrews has come the Law by which the western world has been guided from that day to this.

Nor did the genius of Israel stop there. Great men, great minds, have sprung up throughout all Jewish history, from the kings, judges, and prophets of Bible times to many world-changers of our own time—Sigmund Freud, who revealed to mankind the secrets of our own nature, Albert Einstein, who carried the world from the industrial into the atomic age, and many more, including over thirty Nobel Prize winners.

We Jews have always felt close to our God. We have resisted at all costs the efforts of other nations to deprive us of that spiritual power which has brought us through terrible trials, not without losses but with final victory in our hands.

It is your special blessing as a Jewish girl that you can become one more golden link in the six-thousand-year old chain of Jewish life. For Judaism is not experienced in the synagogue only. Judaism is lived in the home. We may go to the synagogue on Sabbath and holy days, but it is when we come home and find that mother has lit the candles and blessed them, and we sense the atmosphere of peace and festivity in the house, that the holy day really begins. All the life of the home depends upon the wife and mother, for no matter how modern, how independent women may be, the home is still the woman's domain and her responsibility.

But perhaps there is a question in your mind. Perhaps you are thinking that, after all, the Jews, having begun as an oriental nation, still have the attitude that woman is the inferior sex, and that you, as a true Jewish woman and wife, would have to lose something of your own individuality and pride. It may be true of other oriental peoples, but in regard to the Jews it is so far from being true, that in very fact, the opposite is the case! Not only has the Hebrew wife and mother from earliest times had the deciding word in the home, but she was never limited to the home, never shut into the home. Men were allowed more than one wife in some cases, because primitive Hebrew life was a bitter struggle with the soil, and required very large families to cope with it,—but there was never a harem, where women were shut up as in a prison, with no object or use in life but to please the one man who owned them. Even though King Solomon was supposed to have had many wives, they were almost all princesses of foreign nations with whom he gained treaties of peace by marital alliance.

As to the freedom of the married woman outside her home, one example is enough,—that of Deborah, the woman who became chief judge of Israel. The story is told in the Book of Judges without the slightest expression of surprise; it is taken for granted that since this "mother in Israel" is the wisest person in the land, the people choose her as their judge. The general, Barak, doesn't hesitate to ask Deborah to come with him and his army to the battle against the Philistines; in fact, he tells her quite openly that if she won't come along to advise him, he won't undertake the battle!

It is also said that the Hebrew girl was not allowed to choose her husband, that her marriage was arranged for her, even against her will. Well, let us consider the case of Isaac and Rebecca. Abraham felt it so important that his son Isaac should marry the right wife, that he sent his servant Eliezer on a long journey to the city of Nahor. Here Eliezer thought not of the beauty of the hoped-for bride, but of her kindness and intelligence. When he asked Rebecca's family to let her marry Isaac, they said, "We will call Rebecca and ask her." And they asked Rebecca, "Wilt thou go with this man (to wed Isaac)?" And she said, "I will go."

47

The Fifth Commandment says, "Thou shalt honor thy father and thy mother." No difference is made between them. The Book of Proverbs urges, "Obey the command of thy father, and forget not the teaching of thy mother." The husbands are here emphatically warned against turning away from the "wife of thy youth," and urged to avoid "the other woman, for her path is the way of death." Wisdom and industry are represented in Hebrew as feminine. The Book of Proverbs concludes with a song of praise for the true Hebrew housewife, not merely for her beauty and charm but for her strength, her business competence, her intelligence, her tact, her capacity to organize the household.

To live as a true Jewish woman will bring you self-respect, security and peace. To live usefully—knowing that while part of your life is rightly private and personal, the rest of it is to be lived for others—will bring you the sense of being needed, without which no one can be really happy. It is, in fact, woman's discovery that one's own life is part of the life of others, for she is the mother.

For the Jewish woman especially, her usefulness must extend beyond her own family. As long as there are Jewish children waiting to be taught, to be fed, to be clothed, there must be organizations of Jewish women to make sure that these needs are being satisfied.

As long as the state of Israel, which receives so many displaced and suffering Jewish families and individuals, needs to be helped, Jewish women must be part of Israel's resources, bringing that help either by individual efforts or through groups. And in America, as in every country of the world, there are hospitals to be built and staffed, schools to be organized, suffering people to be sought out and aided.

Not all of us can or need be nation-savers or world-shakers, but we should all seek to be of service, if only for our own sakes, for the really unhappy woman is the selfish woman. We may not know any heroines, but we all know and remember with love those women—of whom there are many among the Jews—who give kindness, hospitality, sympathy, warmth, to all who come. To be such a woman is to be a true Jewess.

You as a Jewish daughter are a golden link in the eternal chain of Israel. It is your gift and your privilege, if you so choose, to forge your individual link so that it will be a strong and beautiful ornament in that chain, to be passed on, in due time, to your own daughter and to your daughter's daughter, and so forever, to the end of days.

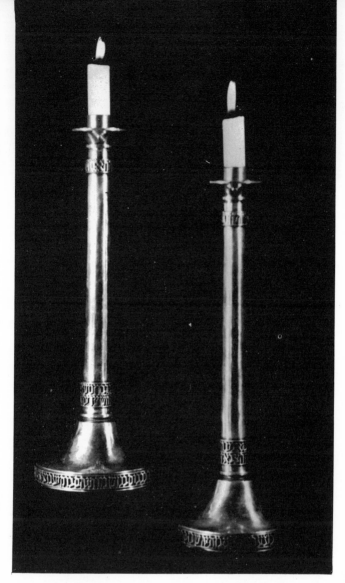

REMEMBER THE SABBATH

Remember the sabbath day, to keep it holy. Six days
shalt thou labour, and do all thy work; but the
seventh day is a sabbath unto the Lord thy God, in
it thou shalt not do any manner of work, thou, nor
thy son, nor thy daughter, nor thy man-servant, nor
thy maid-servant, nor thy cattle, nor thy stranger that
is within thy gates; for in six days the Lord made
heaven and earth, the sea, and all that in them is,
and rested on the seventh day; wherefore the Lord
blessed the sabbath day, and hallowed it.

Exod. 20: 8-11

And the heaven and the earth were finished, and all
the host of them. And on the seventh day God finished His work which He had made; and He rested
on the seventh day from all His work which He had
made. And God blessed the seventh day, and
hallowed it; because that in it He rested from all
His work which God in creating had made.

Gen. 2: 1-3

Wherefore the children of Israel shall keep the
sabbath, to observe the sabbath throughout their
generations, for a perpetual covenant. It is a sign between Me and the children of Israel for ever; for in
six days the Lord made heaven and earth, and on
the seventh day He ceased from work and rested.

Exod. 31: 16-17

KIDDUSH CUP (from Frankfort Synagogue) Frankfort—on—the— Main, Germany, 1600. Gold. Inscriptions from Exodus and Deuteronomy. Recovered with other Nazi loot by The Jewish Cultural Reconstruction, Inc., and in 1951 given to The Jewish Museum, New York City

KIDDUSH CUP FOR THE SYNAGOGUE,
by William B. Meyers, Newark, N. J.
Silver with bead edges and grape cluster
ornamentations; bowl lined with gold.
Courtesy, Union of American Hebrew Congregations, New York

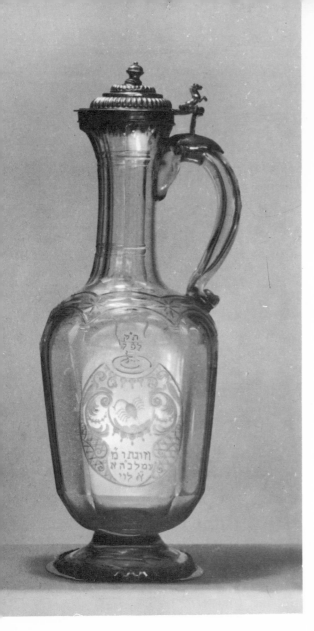

KIDDUSH CUP, Augsberg, Germany, 18th century
Silver, gilded and chased. Inscription:
"Remember the Sabbath Day to keep it holy.
Remember it with a blessing over wine."
Courtesy, The Jewish Museum, New York City

NE CARAFE, Moravia, 1740, Bezalel Museum, Jerusalem.
rtesy, American Fund for Israel Institutions

PLATE FOR WINE CUP by Ilya Schor. Silver, engraved and appliqued, with inscription giving the blessing over the wine.
Courtesy, Dr. and Mrs. A. Kanof, Brooklyn, New York

"THE FATHER RETURNS FROM THE SYNAGOGUE ON FRIDAY EVENING" Woodcut by Ilya Schor
Midrashic lore relates that two angels, one good, the other bad, accompany the father on his return from
the synagogue. The sanctity and delight of the Sabbath in the home overwhelms the bad angel who,
against his will, responds "Amen" to the father's chanting of "Shalom Aleichem."

The only festive observance ordered by the Ten Commandments is that of the
Sabbath (*Shabbat*). The greatness of the day is stressed in all the sacred writings
of Israel. In the Talmud we read: "The Holy One, blessed is He, spake unto Moses,
'I have a precious gift in my treasure house, and Sabbath is its name. I wish to
present it to Israel. Go and bring them the good tidings."

This day of rest and holiness was not only a gift to Israel. It was the first time in
human history that every seventh day was set aside for sanctity and repose. Some
nations of antiquity had no rest days whatever. Other religions derived from Judaism, though observing a different day of the week, adapted the Sabbath idea from the
Jews. When the leaders of the French Revolution tried to overturn previous custom and employ the decimal system even in matters of work cessation, making
every tenth day the period of rest, they found it necessary to return to the custom
of the seventh day rest. They discovered that one out of seven was the minimum required by any worker to do his best and preserve his health.

There are two versions of the Ten Commandments in the Bible. In the first
(Exodus 20) we are enjoined: "Remember the Sabbath day, to keep it holy . . . .
for in six days the Lord made heaven and earth, the sea, and all that in them is, and
rested on the seventh day; wherefore the Lord blessed the Sabbath day, and

hallowed it." In the variant (Deuteronomy 5) we read: "Observe the Sabbath day, to keep it holy . . . . And thou shalt remember that thou wast a servant in the land of Egypt, and the Lord thy God brought thee out of thence . . . . therefore the Lord thy God commanded thee to keep the sabbath day."

From these declarations we understand that men are to rest from all their weekday activities — but not solely because physical rest is a human necessity. Thought must be directed to God and His creation. By remembering the cruel enslavement of man by man, each person attains a social attitude toward all others. He recognizes the importance of social justice, of freedom and understanding. For one God is the creator of all things and of all men. When men find respite from the toil and turmoil of the week, they should contemplate things of the spirit — study, prayer, introspection.

To the Jew the benefits of the Sabbath must be extended to all persons with whom he has any relationship whatever. "In it thou shalt not do any manner of work, thou, nor thy son, nor thy daughter, nor thy man-servant, nor thy maid-servant, nor thy cattle, nor thy stranger that is within thy gates" — so that they "may rest as well as thou." Here is the first expression of Jewish universalism, disclosing the biblical inclusion of all God's children in the teachings and traditions and practices of Judaic social justice.

. . . ."And call the Sabbath a delight."   Is. 58:13.

"SABBATH REST" by Moritz Oppenheim, "

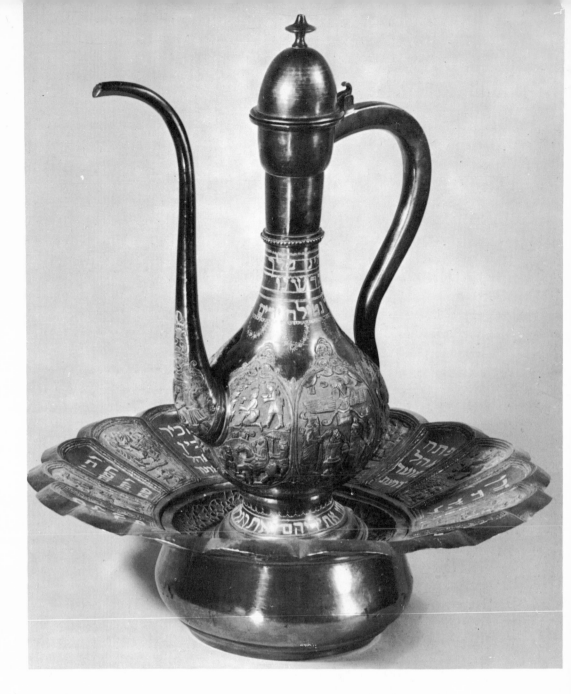

PITCHER, Oriental, late 18th century. Silver, hammered, and engraved.
Courtesy, collection of Louis S. Werner, New York City.

During most of the centuries of Jewish life, the people of Israel observed the
Sabbath to the fullest. The best foods, the best clothes, the best of everything, were
reserved for the holy day. The laws designed to prevent infractions of full rest were
scrupulously observed. No power could weaken the Jewish resolve to sanctify
the day. The Talmud tells of a Roman emperor who boasted that he was as powerful as God. A Jewish sage suggested that he order all fires to be extinguished on a

54

certain day. Yet from the palace one could see wisps of smoke from many chimneys. Said the sage, "Your majesty, you have immediate power of life and death over your subjects. Yet they disobey you. But God ordered the Jews not to kindle flame on the Sabbath; and when you look at the Jewish homes on that day you will find none in which this command was broken."

So strong has been the influence of the Sabbath in shaping the life and destiny of the Jewish people.

The idea of the seventh day was extended far beyond the limits of the week. The Torah commanded that all slaves be freed and compensated after seven years, to assume the roles of free men. On the jubilee year, not only were slaves to be liberated, but all real property that had been sold was to revert to the former owners — thus equalizing the general economy.

Everything done during the week is by the Jews considered anticipatory and preparatory for the Sabbath. The other days have no names in the Hebrew calendar, only numbers (first day, second day) — they advance progressively to the final sanctity of *Shabbat*. Great preparations are made in the home; since there can be no cooking on the Sabbath itself, all food for the traditional three meals is ready before nightfall on Friday, when the candles are blessed by the mother of the household. Thus the house is already sanctified while the male worshipers are at the synagogue.

At the synagogue the day is greeted lovingly, bearing the poetic figures of "Queen" and "Bride." Before the common evening prayers are recited, there is a service of *Kabbalat Shabbat*, welcoming the Sabbath. This contains an acrostic hymn for Friday eve by Rabbi Solomon Halevi Alkabetz (16c.), with the refrain, "Come, my friend, to meet the bride; let us welcome the presence of the Sabbath."

Kiddush, or the Sabbath and festival sanctification over wine, is first recited at the synagogue. For in ancient and even comparatively recent days travelers and poor folk ate and slept in the vestry rooms, making the house of worship their temporary home.

The returning worshipers find their home and table spiritually and physically glorified. The candles gleam; the table is set with a handsome cloth; all is prepared for the symbolic Queen. The father chants a hymn to the heavenly beings: "Come in peace, angels of peace, messengers from on high." He blesses his children, and chants the thirty-first chapter of Proverbs, exalting the woman of worth and valor. The evening is a time for rest at home, or some study of sacred lore.

The custom of studying the biblical portion of the week is carried out in the morning before the family leaves for the synagogue. At the synagogue there is a morning service *(Shaharit),* followed by the formal reading of the weekly portion of the Torah and related chapters from the Prophets. Thus, during the year, the entire Pentateuch (Five Books of Moses), is certain to be read — an achievement

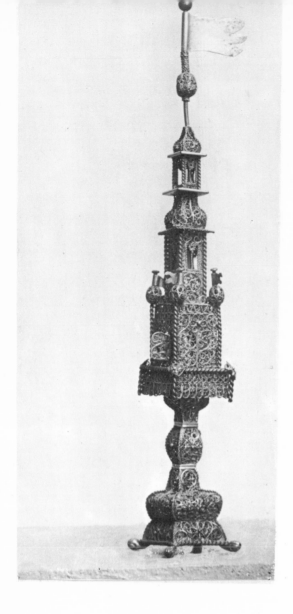

SPICE CONTAINER by William B. Meyers, Newark, N. J. Silver, bead edge and grape cluster ornamentation. Courtesy, Union of Hebrew Congregations, New York City

SPICE CONTAINER (tower form), 17th century, Silver filigree. In Bezalel Museum, Jerusalem. Courtesy, American Fund for Israel Institutions

celebrated on the festival of *Simhat Torah.* Then comes *Musaf* (an additional service) which generally is concluded with a hymn glorifying the Creator of the universe.

The noon meal is also preceded by a *kiddush.* A third meal (*Shalosh Seudot*) is prescribed for the period between the afternoon (*Minhah*) and evening (*Maariv*) services. When the evening prayer is concluded after nightfall, the *Havdalah* ("division") blessing is chanted over wine to mark the separation of the Sabbath from the weekdays, and the beginning of a new and, we hope, of a "good week." In addition to the blessing over wine, there are benedictions over spice (in a special container of wood or metal), since spice was used at the end of a meal in olden days; and over candle or other light, since now it is permitted once more to kindle lights. At home *Havdalah* is recited by the father for the benefit of all the family.

HAVDALAH SET, by H. David Gumbel, contemporary Israeli silversmith. Silver, with cutout Hebrew lettering, In Bezalel Museum, Jerusalem.
Courtesy, American Fund for Israel Institutions

Sabbath observances were never considered a hardship or limitation by religious Jews. They are the means for proper exaltation of the holiest day and of the "additional soul" each observant Jew is presumed to have gained with the Sabbath advent.

On the Sabbath *Zemirot*, songs expressing the spirit of the day, and hymns are chanted at the table. A free rendition of one of these is — *Yom Zeh Mechubad* ("*Honored is this day*"):

> This day above all other days is blessed,
> For on it did the Lord God choose to rest.
> Six days in toil and work are spent;
> The seventh day for God is meant.
> So cease from toil; crown His intent
> Who made the world at His behest.
> The heavens e'er proclaim God's praise;
> The earth His love and grace displays.
> He made all creatures, rules their ways;
> Perfection, all His works attest.

There are specially named Sabbaths in the Jewish year, on which variant readings from the Torah and the Prophets are substituted.

The first Sabbath after *Simhat Torah* is called *Shabbat Bereshit*, which is the first Hebrew word in the Bible — for then the reading of the Torah begins anew.

Shabbat Shirah ("song") is that on which the portion *Beshallah*, containing the Song of Moses, is read. This Sabbath generally comes in *Shevat* (early February).

On *Shabbat Shekalim*, which occurs in Adar (late February), there is an additional reading concerning the prescribed giving of the shekel.

The Sabbath before Purim is *Shabbat Zakhor*, after the Torah reading — which begins *Zakhor* ("Remember") what Amalek did.

On the Sabbath after Purim the laws of the red heifer *("parah")* are read, hence it is called *Shabbat Parah*.

Shabbat ha-Hodesh ("the month") is celebrated just before the first of *Nisan*, month of Passover.

Before Tish ah B'av comes *Shabbat Hazon*, so named after the first word in Isaiah (prophetic reading of that Sabbath.) After Tish ah B'Av comes *Shabbat Nahamu*, for the first word in Isaiah 40 (the Sabbath's *haftarah*) — "Comfort ye, my people."

Shabbat Teshuvah is the one between *Rosh Hashanah* and *Yom Kippur*. Any Sabbath coinciding with the New Moon is called *Shabbat Rosh Hodesh*. (Sukkot — The Feast of Tabernacles, the Season of Our Gladness)

ROSH HASHANAH

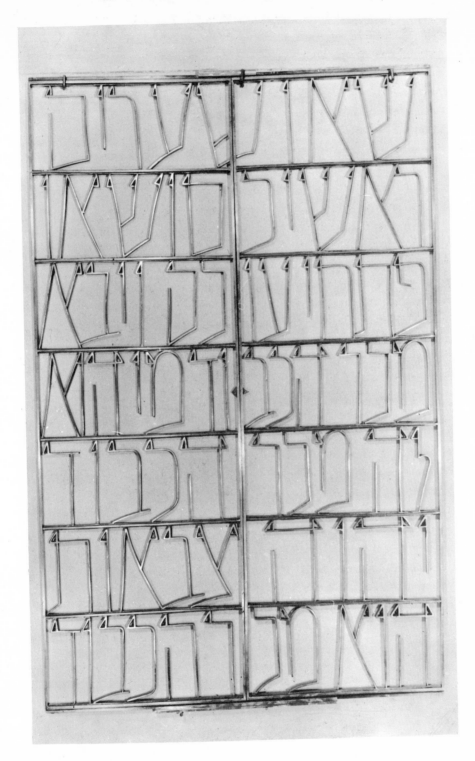

DOORS FOR THE HOLY TORAH ARK
Brass, formed of modern Hebrew lettering, the text taken from Chapter 24 of Psalms, " . . . lift up your heads, O ye gates . . . that the King of Glory may come in . . . " In the Bezalel Museum, Jerusalem
Courtesy, American Fund for Israel Institutions

The first day of the Hebrew month *Tishri*, which comes in the fall, is the Jewish New Year. The name *Rosh Hashanah* ("head of the year") is not given in the Bible, which calls it instead *Yom Teruah* or *Zichron Teruah* — "day of sounding the shofar" or "memorial of the sounding of the shofar" (ram's horn). Other names, found in our holiday prayerbook, are *Yom ha-Zikkaron* and *Yom ha-Din* — "day of memorial" and "day of judgment." The Jewish New Year has a variety of meanings and observances, and each of its names refers to a special significance.

After the Exodus from Egypt, the month of *Nissan*, on which Passover occurs, was generally accepted as Israel's first month. But it appears that in the earliest days *Tishri* was first. The difficulties in establishing the calendar, already mentioned, extended the observance from one to two days; and even in Israel, which observes but one instead of two days on other holidays, the two days of *Rosh Hashanah* are retained. The Hebrew word for repentance is *teshuvah* — "turning" — denoting the genuine change of heart which impels the sinner to turn from evil, and return to God. *Rosh Hashanah* begins a ten day period of repentance, during which "the remembrance of every creature, man's deeds and destiny, his works and ways, his thoughts and designs" are forcefully brought to mind. And since recalling the missteps of the year past creates problems of conscience, *Rosh Hashanah* adds to the thought of memory the idea of judgment. Each man must judge his own actions, and take steps to eradicate personal sins and errors as well as injuries done one's fellowman. God will forgive or punish transgressions against Him as He sees fit; our primary concern is to conduct ourselves in a Godly manner toward our brethren on earth, who are all God's children.

The outstanding and best remembered custom of *Rosh Hashanah* is the sounding of the *shofar*, whose weird notes from the oldest of wind instruments are designed to awaken all worshipers to the need for prayer and repentance. The *shofar* was sounded at Mount Sinai; it was employed to herald the year of jubilee. It proclaimed many other historical and ritual observances, and it was used as a warning of immediate danger.

There are one hundred blasts prescribed in the *mahzor* (holiday prayerbook). They are heard in the latter portions of the morning services, probably because children and laggards will all be present during the final hours. The notes announced before each sounding are *tekiah*, the single blast; *shevarim*, a three-part broken blast; and *teruah*, a rapid succession of short notes. All the notes are calculated to rouse men's consciences, bring searching of hearts, and assure meditation on improving one's way in life. The ram's horn is used because, when Abraham was about to express his supreme faith by offering up his son Isaac, it was a ram caught in the bushes which became the substitute sacrifice.

On the day when all mankind is to pass in judgment before God, it also

ROSH HASHANAH PLATE, Holland, circa 1700
Faience, blue and white
On the eve of the New Year used for serving an apple dipped in honey
Courtesy, The Jewish Museum, New York City

expresses every important teaching and future hope of the people of Israel. Saadia Gaon (892-942) saw in the *shofar* blast intimations of the following episodes to God, the revelation on Mount Sinai, and duties: the Creation, the sinner's return the exhortations of the prophets, the destruction of the Temple, Abraham's binding of Isaac for the sacrifice, alertness to peril, conscience and judgment, Israel's redemption, and life eternal.

61

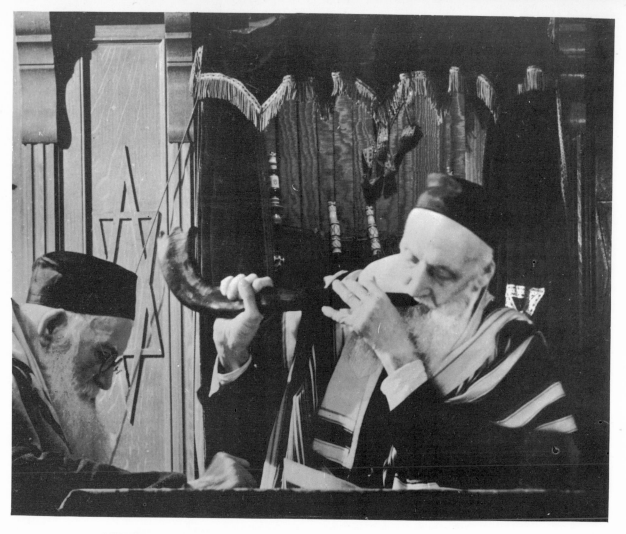

SOUNDING THE SHOFAR
" . . . Shall the shofar be blown in the city, and the people not tremble?" *Amos 3:6*

Rosh Hashanah prayers recognize the truth that man is frail, and always in need of repentance for past misdeeds. They dramatize the Jewish precept that man must take continuous stock of himself and his acts, and not only on days set aside for that purpose. We are exhorted by our liturgy to find the blame for our hardships in ourselves — but we add a note of hopefulness to our plaints. For ultimately "the upright will be glad . . . . and Thou shalt remove the dominion of evil from the earth."

At meals on *Rosh Hashanah* bread is dipped in honey as a symbol of a sweeter and better year to come. A new fruit is tasted, so as further to justify our thanks to God for giving us life to this time and renewing our spiritual power. Sin in itself is overpowering; and one widely practised custom is that of *tashlikh* — the "casting away" of sin, through symbolic rites by a running stream.

Many special hymns and poems are recited on *Rosh Hashanah*, most of them composed during medieval times. The most important of these, read also on *Yom*

Kippur, is *Unetaneh Tokef*, composed by Rabbi Amnon of Mayence. According to the story related in the centuries following, Amnon was pressed by the local bishop to accept conversion. Once, instead of an immediate refusal to follow the bishop's behest, he begged for three days to consider. For this hesitation he felt so guilty that when summoned to the bishop's presence he asked that his tongue be cut off. Instead, the priest had the rabbi's hands and feet amputated. As the story continues, Rabbi Amnon requested to be brought into the synagogue. When the *kedushah*, or sanctification service read by cantor and congregation, was about to begin, he asked permission to offer a prayer he had written. Immediately afterward, he passed away.

Rabbi Amnon's prayer, which gives expression to the mystic idea inherent in the *Rosh Hashanah* services, may well close any description of the Jewish New Year:

"We will celebrate the mighty holiness of this day, a day of awe and terror, a day on which Thy Kingdom is exalted and Thy throne established in mercy, on which Thou sittest in truth. Verily Thou art the judge and arbiter Who knowest all, and bearest witness, and writest and sealest and recordest, and reckonest. Thou rememberest all forgotten things. Thou openest the Book of Records from which the accounting is read, attested by the seal of every man. A great trumpet is sounded, and a still, small voice is heard. Even the angels are dismayed, for fear and trembling have seized them, as they proclaim: This is the day of judgment whereon the heavenly host is arraigned in judgment, for even they are not pure in Thine eyes; and all who enter the world Thou dost cause to pass before Thee as a flock of sheep. Yea, even as a shepherd mustereth his flock and passeth his lambs beneath the crook, so dost Thou cause to pass, and number and count and visit, every living soul, appointing to each of Thy creatures the measure of their days and writing down their destiny.

"On the New Year it is written, and on the Day of Atonement it is sealed, how many are to pass away and how many to be born; who shall live and who shall die; to whom shall be granted the full time allotted to man and who shall be taken before his course is run; who is to perish by fire and who by water; who by the sword and who by wild beasts; who by hunger and who by thirst; who by earthquake and who by plague; who by strangling and who by stoning; who shall be at rest and who displaced; who shall be tranquil and who disturbed; who shall be at ease and who chastened; who shall become poor and who enriched; who shall be abased and who uplifted.

"BUT PENITENCE, PRAYER, AND CHARITY AVERT THE EVIL DECREE!"

DAYS OF PENITENCE

There are ten days of *teshuvah* — "turning" or "penitence" — beginning with *Rosh Hashanah* and ending with *Yom Kippur*. During all this time the spiritual stocktaking enjoined upon every Jew must continue. For the rabbis understood that taking account of our conduct and altering our future for the better are not easy tasks. Men are creatures of habit, even when they are aware that the habits are bad and destructive. To the teachers of Israel there could never be too much *teshuvah*.

The *asseret yeme teshuvah*, this important ten-day period, is to be approached with three aims — abandonment of the wrongful path, honest remorse, and an active effort to achieve atonement by good deeds. The Talmud tells of three books being opened in heaven. One is for the completely righteous, who are at once inscribed in the book of life; another is for the wholly wicked, who are in the book of the condemned. The third is for the great mass of indeterminate humans whose doom is suspended during these ten days; and according to his deserts each is then inscribed in the book of life or is condemned.

The Sabbath falling within the ten days is called *Shabbat Shuvah*, since the prophetic reading for the day begins with the words. *Shuvah Yisrael* — "Return, O Israel, unto the Lord thy God." It has been the custom for rabbis to deliver lengthy discourses on human life and morals on this Sabbath.

There are insertions in the congregational prayers throughout the period, which briefly plead for the worshiper's inclusion in the book of life. A series of supplications each beginning *Avinu Malkenu* — "Our Father, our King" — is recited twice a day.

And it shall come to pass in the end of days,

That the mountain of the Lord's house shall be established

  as the top of the mountains,

And shall be exalted above the hills;

And all nations shall flow unto it.

And many peoples shall go and say:

'Come ye, and let us go up to the mountain of the Lord,

To the house of the God of Jacob;

And He will teach us of His ways,

And we will walk in His paths.'

For out of Zion shall go forth the law,

And the word of the Lord from Jerusalem.

And He shall judge between the nations,

And shall decide for many peoples;

And they shall beat their swords into plowshares

And their spears into pruning-hooks;

Nation shall not lift up sword against nation,

Neither shall they learn war any more.

                      Isaiah 2:2-4

"AND THEY SHALL BEAT THEIR SWORDS INTO PLOWSHARES . . . " *(Is. 2:4)*
Sculpture by Moissaye Marans, Brooklyn, New York
Reproduced through courtesy of the Architectural League, New York City

YOM KIPPUR

Yom Kippur, which climaxes the ten days of penitence, is observed by fasting and prayer for over twenty-four hours. The Bible orders all Jews to "afflict" themselves during this day of repentance, and affliction has been expounded as abstaining from food, the least harmful of possible self-injuries. After eating a festive meal in broad daylight, the worshiper arrives at the synagogue while it is still light. He leaves the house of worship the next evening after dark, following recital of the regular evening prayer. Except where illness prevents, or the person is too young or too old, no food or drink is taken through the entire period.

Yet at no time is there anything fearsome about the Day of Atonement. The worshiper feels that he is carrying out one of the finest behests of his religion. The same restraint of appetite applying to food, can be translated to conduct conducive to sin. The penitent learns that will power can overcome temptation, and this lesson is applied to his daily conduct.

Throughout the service it is stressed that *Yom Kippur* atones only for sins against God, "but for transgressions against a fellowman the Day of Atonement does not atone, unless and until he has conciliated his fellowman, and redressed the wrong he has done him."

Quite naturally the outstanding day of the Jewish year must have many unique customs. Men wear *kittels* (white gowns) representing the ideal of purity. Shoes are removed, to emulate the custom of the ancient priests when they trod holy ground. There are special blessings for one's children and other distinctive acts.

Nothing in the day's customs and liturgy even remotely approaches the uniqueness of the extraordinary special service for the first moments of the fastday, known as *Kol Nidre* ("All vows"). This is chanted three times, beginning while there still is light. It is sung to one of the most distinctive melodies known to man, plaintive, beautiful, appealing. This prayer was composed in the early centuries of the present era. Long after, when Spain persecuted the Jews under Ferdinand

and Isabella, on *Yom Kippur*, these forced converts (known as Marranos,) would assemble in secret. The elders would then declare that the false oaths imposed upon the congregation were null and void, like any vow made under compulsion. The music was composed to fit the words. Later the custom spread to other lands.

In certain communities of the ninth and tenth centuries, particularly in Arabia, there is no record of the *Kol Nidre* being sung on *Yom Kippur*. But in Spain, where the words originated, the prayer was recited all through the so-called Golden Age under the Moslems. It became significant once more when new persecutions arose in that country. And under the Christian persecutions of Ferdinand and Isabella there was more reason than ever to proclaim the abrogation of forced vows at secret *Yom Kippur* services.

"BETH HAMIDRASH" oil by Isidor Kaufman
Courtesy, Oscar Gruss, New York City

There are two sentences that precede the cantor's rendition of *Kol Nidre*. One is the phrase from Psalms—"Light is sown for the righteous, and gladness for the upright in heart." This is the principle behind all prayers for repentance, which bring light and gladness to all devout men. The other phrase was devised to silence such members of the congregation as might protest the admission into the synagogue of Marranos who had chosen to masquerade as Christians in Spain. Many of these Jews seeking reconversion fled to Amsterdam, Hamburg, and other more northern communities, were the elders devised a formula to silence the objectors: "With the consent of God, and with consent of the congregation, by authority of the court on high, and by authority of the court on earth, we give leave to pray with them that have transgressed."

It must not be forgotten that the oaths from which men could thus be absolved did not cover transgressions against fellowmen, but only those against God and His Law. But many Jew-haters attempted to prove that *Kol Nidre* was a blanket permission for all Jews to violate any promises made to their fellows. It was sometimes necessary to recite an introduction to the prayer clarifying its intent.

There are two "confessionals" in the *Yom Kippur* prayers—*Ashamnu* and *Al Het*—recited several times during the services. Since every possible sin is confessed to God, even by those who have committed no sin whatever, and since the plural is used throughout, the confession is completely impersonal. It covers all the sins of all the congregation, yet no one can ascertain the particular crimes committed by any individual.

Numerous impressive hymns—*piyyutim*—appear in the service of the cantor and congregation. In the additional morning service (*Mussaf*) the *Avodah* (service of the high priest in ancient days) is described in poetic form. The reading from the Torah in the morning applies to the *Yom Kippur* sacrifices in the Temple. The prophetic reading immediately following is from Isaiah 57: it stresses penitence, humility, and peace. There is an added Torah reading during the afternoon service, which consists of the laws of forbidden marriage; on this day the importance of sex morality is strongly proclaimed. The *haftarah*, or prophetic reading, consists mainly of the entire Book of Jonah—for the story of the prophet who fled from God's bidding and then repented illustrates the power and worth of sincere atonement for sin.

Just before the sun begins to set, the special and final *Yom Kippur* service called *Neilah*—"closing"— is chanted. Before the "gates of heaven" are closed, the worshippers pray that they may be "sealed" in the book of life. The day is ended with a final blast of the *shofar*, acceptance of the unity of God, and a hope for restoration of the Holy City of Jerusalem.

"THE SUKKAH" by Moritz Oppenheim, Germany (1800-1882)
"Thou shalt keep the Feast of Tabernacles . . ."
Courtesy, Oscar Gruss, New York City

Two weeks after *Rosh Hashanah,* five days after *Yom Kippur,* begin the nine days known as *Sukkot.* This word means tabernacles or booths — for the ancestors of Israel wandered for long years in the desert, living in booths or temporary huts, before reaching the Promised Land and achieving their independent nationhood. In Leviticus 23:34 we read "on the fifteenth day of this seventh month is the feast of tabernacles for seven days unto the Lord"; and "Ye shall dwell in booths seven days . . . . that your generations may know that I made the children of Israel to dwell in booths, when I brought them out of the land of Egypt" (Lev. 23:42, 43).

Insomuch as the *sukkah* built in the centuries thereafter by observant Jews was to be a symbol of God's goodness in times of stress, and of the faith that sustained the wanderers, each hut has to conform with certain stringent rules. It must be not higher than twenty cubits (about thirty feet), nor lower than ten handbreadths — teaching that man should become neither overly haughty nor excessively humble and subservient. There must be more shade than sun, as a means for intensifying the lessons of steadfastness and humility, as distinct from the misleading glare of the world at large. The latticed roof may be covered only with broken leaves and branches, through which the stars may be seen. These are reminders of Israel's eternal Guardian. And within are hung fruits and vegetables, indicating the bounties of the Lord.

Since this is the season of the harvest, the festival is also known as *Hag he-Asif,* Feast of the Ingathering. The Lord is thanked at religious services not only through prayer, but through the use of four species ordained by the Bible itself. We bring together the *etrog,* or citron; the *lulav,* palm branch; *hadassim,* myrtle; and *aravot,* willow, both as agricultural symbols and as representing the four kinds of men making up the nation, or any nation. According to the Midrash, the *etrog* has both taste and a good odor, signifying those who are both learned and religiously observant. The *lulav* has fruit that can be eaten, but no fragrance — like the learned ones who do not carry out the precepts of their faith. The myrtle, which has a good odor but no taste, is like the men of good and pious deeds who possess no scholarship. And the willow, lacking both food value and fragrance, refers to such as have neither learning nor good deeds.

Every day but the Sabbath the four species are part of the religious service. At prescribed times they are pointed in all directions, thus proclaiming the dominion of God in all places on earth. Carrying these four species, worshipers make circuits *(hakafot)* within the synagogue — chanting prayers of praise, thanksgiving, and trust in the Lord.

Now in olden days it was declared that on this festival judgment was passed on the coming of rain. Hence in the Land of Israel there was a brilliant colorful ceremony of water drawing — *simhat bet ha-shoevah* — fully described in the Talmud, and now being reenacted in the new State. And every seven years, com-

SUKKAH WITH WALL PAINTING, Bavaria, circa 1820.
After World War II the original wooden boards were sent to Jerusalem from Bavaria and reconstructed in
the Jewish National Museum, Bezalel. Note photograph of interior of *sukkah* for close-up of wall
paintings of German and Jerusalem landscapes.

"BLESSING ON TAKING THE LULAV" pen and ink by H. Felix Kraus, New York

mands the Bible, Israel is to assemble (*hakhel*) on *Sukkot* for instruction. For the first time in centuries such a celebration was conducted in the new Israel during *Sukkot* of 1952.

The seventh day of *Sukkot* is known as *Hoshana Rabba,* because of the large number of chants beginning with the word *hoshana* (save!) that mark the special processions within the synagogue. Willow branches are then beaten, until all leaves are broken off — symbolizing the hope that after the trees and plants lose their leaves God will provide new warmth and moisture for the renewal of nature, man's strength, and man's trust in the Divine.

Then comes *Shemini Atzeret,* the Eighth Day of Solemn Assembly. This is designated by the sages as a distinct festival, not connected with *Sukkot* itself. It is marked by special sacrifices, benedictions, and psalm reading. It is also signalized by special jubilation, although all the days are known as *zeman simhatenu,* the season of our rejoicing. There are dancing and singing, such as Jerusalem witnessed in centuries past. The major feature of the service is the prayer for rain, chanted by the cantor in the same kind of white garment and similar tones employed on *Yom Kippur.* For without rain life could not exist in the land; and the rainy season was

"THE FOUR SPECIES" oil painting by Ilya Schor,
Painting is in the Har Zion Temple, Philadelphia, Pennsylvania

ETHROG CONTAINER by Ilya Schor, New York City
Silver, engraved and appliqued
Courtesy, Siegfried Bendheim, New York City

"SIMHAT TORAH" oil painting by Solomon Alexander Hart (1806-1881), England, 1842. Interior of Synagogue of Livorno, Italy.
Courtesy, Oscar Gruss, New York City.

"This Feast of the law all your gladness
*   display,*
*   Today all your homages render.*
What profit can lead one so pleasant a
*   way,*
*   What jewels can vie with its splendor?*
Then exult on the Law on its festival
*   day;*
*   The Law is our light and defender."*

"SIMHAT TORAH" woodcut by Ilya Schor, New York City

always welcomed with prayer and gladness. On this day Jews throughout the world begin to interpolate in the *Shemoneh Esreh* (Eighteen Benediction) prayer the phrase, "Thou causest the wind to blow and the rain to fall."

The ninth day is known as *Simhat Torah* — Rejoicing of the Law — (in Israel it is observed together with *Shemini Atzeret*). The joy is created by the fact that on this day the annual Sabbath reading of the Five Books of Moses is completed, and the new cycle begun. The Torah, which has been called a "traveling fatherland," has been the guide and protection of the people of Israel through all their hardships and wanderings. At the services all the Torah scrolls are taken from the Ark and borne about the synagogue, with song and dance — both in the evening and the morning. Every man has the honor of ascending to the reading of the scrolls, even the young lads, reciting the proper benedictions.

There are two special honors accorded those called to the reading. The person to whom is assigned the final passage of the Torah is the *Hatan Torah* — bridegroom of the Torah. He who begins the reading of the Five Books of Moses anew is known as the *Hatan Bereshit* — bridegroom of Genesis. These honors are customarily given to men of learning and piety, for the close association of the final and initial readings of the Pentateuch are an indication of the eternity of God's revelation and the perpetuity of the people of Israel.

TORAH DRESSED WITH MAN-
TLE, CROWN, BREASTPLATE
AND POINTER

Mantle: Brocade and velvet, Germany, 1765

Crown: Silver, Poland, 18th century

Breastplate: Silver, Galicia, 1870

Pointer: Silver, Galicia, early 19th
century

Courtesy, The Jewish Museum, New
York City

HANUKKAH

After the death of Alexander the Great (323 B.C.E.), and the split-up of the Greek Empire, many of the rulers of Palestine attempted to force the Jews to give up their own religion and customs in favor of the Greek and pagan forms. Some Jews yielded to the powers above them, but most of them refused to become pagans under compulsion. Then a certain cruel king, Antiochus of Syria, determined to use all the power of his position and his armies to destroy the Jewish faith, and to kill those Jews who would not obey his commands.

The thought of worshiping idols or images has always repelled Jews. It is stringently forbidden in the Ten Commandments. Yet Antiochus persisted in setting up statues of Zeus, the chief god of Greece, for the Jews to bow down to. A large image was placed in the Temple of Jerusalem itself. Altars were scattered throughout the land, before which sacrifices were to be offered to the Greek gods. The king forbade observance of the Sabbath, the festivals, or the laws concerning food. Many Jews escaped to the hills and caves; others were put to death by the soldiers. Scrolls of the Torah were destroyed, and their owners killed. The Temple was looted and defiled.

Judas Maccabaeus and his eight hundred warriors defeated in the battle of Elasa after a heroic fight against the superior Seleucid force.
Courtesy, The Harry Levine Foundation

HANUKKAH MENORAH, Germany, early 18th century
Silver with enamel medallions on base
Presented to The Jewish Museum, New York City, by Mrs. Felix M. Warburg, in memory of her father,
Jacob H. Schiff, to whom the lamp belonged.

HANUKKAH DREIDEL

The rebellion began in the little town of Modin. Here a courageous old man named Mattathias struck down a Jew who was obeying a military order to bow down to an idol; and his five sons, led by the famed Judas Maccabeus, slew the soldiers and organized a nationwide revolt. Though vastly outarmed and outnumbered, the Jews defeated the Syrians, and in three years they were again able to enter the holy Temple. This was in the year 165 before the common reckoning.

It is related that there was only one tiny cruse of oil in the structure — seemingly enough for but one day in the sacred eternal lamp. It was the only oil sanctified and sealed by the high priest. But, wondrously enough, it burnt for eight full days! So *Hanukkah,* the Feast of Dedication — or the Feast of Lights — is still celebrated for eight days. It begins on the twenty-fifth of *Kislev,* generally about the middle of December.

In order that all may see and understand the miracle of those ancient days, the candelabrum *(Hanukkiyah)* for the holiday is placed where even those outside may look upon it. As soon as stars appear, the candles (or oil wicks) are kindled with appropriate blessings and hymns. A *shamash* (sexton) or server candle is used to light the first candle, to the far right of the *Hanukkah* lamp. Each night an additional candle is set at the left, the last one being first exposed to the flame. On the eighth night all the candles are illuminated. Altogether, including the "sextons," forty-four are lit during the period.

The consecrated candles may not be used to kindle other candles; therefore the *Shamash,* or server candle, is employed for that purpose. One of the hymns sung is *Maoz Tzur,* known in English as "Rock of Ages."

Hanukkah is important for world history as well, for this marks the first successful insurrection against limitation of religious freedom anywhere in the world. In the words recited in the *Siddur* on the days of Hanukkah *(Al ha-Nissim):* "Thou deliveredst the strong into the hands of the weak, the many into the hands of the few, the impure into the hands of the pure, the wicked into the hands of the righteous, and the arrogant into the hands of them that occupied themselves with Thy Law." It remains an example for all the persecuted and downtrodden peoples of the world, that righteousness and justice will triumph so long as men are dedicated to relighting the flame of God in their homes and their temples.

The Jewish triumph not only preserved Judaism, but thereby paved the way for all modern religion emanating from it.

HANUKKAH LAMPS developed into two distinct types — first, the bench type for use in the home only, the back wall providing the artist with space for decorative ornamentation. The larger Hanukkah menorah was a later development, designed for use in the synagogue . . . . "We kindle these lights on account of the miracles and deliverances and wonders which Thou didst work for our fathers . . . "

MENORAH, Hamburg, 17th century
Courtesy, The Jewish Museum, New York City

THE VICTORY OF THE SPIRIT

Hanukkah, the Feast of the Maccabees, celebrates a victory — not a military victory only, but a victory also of the spirit — over things material. Not a victory only over external enemies, the Greeks; but a victory also over more dangerous internal enemies. A victory of the many over the ease-loving, safe-playing, privileged, powerful few, who in their pliancy would have betrayed the best interests of the people, a victory of democracy over aristocracy.

As part of the eternal world-wide struggle for democracy, the struggle of the Maccabees is of eternal worldwide interest. It is a struggle of the Jews of today as well as of those of two thousand years ago. It is a struggle in which all Americans, non-Jews as well as Jews, should be vitally interested because they are vitally affected.

The Maccabees' victory proved that the Jews — then already an old people — possessed the secret of eternal youth: the ability to rejuvenate itself through courage, hope, enthusiasm, devotion, and self-sacrifice of the plain people.

Louis D. Brandeis (1856-1941)

MENORAH-TOPPED LOOKOUT TOWER
RISES TO THE SKIES, ISRAEL
Courtesy, Jewish National Fund, New York

THE DAY OF CARNAGE

From the beginning of the siege of Jerusalem by the Babylonians in 588 B.C.E. through the slaughter of six million Jews by the Nazis during the second World War, stretches a long period of suffering and ruthless extermination. The beginning of this series of holocausts is marked by a fast day on the tenth of Teveth (Asarah be'Teveth). On that day began the siege of Jerusalem by Nebuchadnezzar. It was fitting that this day should also be designated by world Jewry to commemorate the slaughter of the last war. The destruction of the great Eastern and Central European Jewish civilization was the culminating tragedy of the process begun by the Babylonians almost 2,600 years ago.

This catastrophe, marked officially by the fast day of Asarah be'Teveth, has already become the subject of a vast literature. In Hebrew it is referred to as *Hashoah*, the fearful destruction. As the story unfolds — in books, in memoirs, poetry, and fiction — we catch glimpses of the heroic spirit of Israel in the face of almost certain death. Hitler destroyed the bodies of millions of our brethren, but their spirit he could not cremate. In countless acts of resistance, culminating in the heroic Warsaw uprising, doomed Jews showed their kinship with the heroic forefathers who had defied the brutalitarians of their age — Babylonians, Assyrians, Greeks, Romans, Nazis.

May their memory ever recall the greatness of the prophet's vision of a united humanity, for which they gave their lives.

CHIEF RABBI OF ISRAEL, DR. ISAAC HERZOG, PLANTING THE FIRST TREE IN THE FOREST OF THE SIX MILLION MARTYRS, ISRAEL
Courtesy, Jewish National Fund, New York

יער הקדושים

MARTYRS' FOREST

MARTYRS' FOREST, ISRAEL, Poster
Courtesy, Jewish National Fund, New York

THE LAST DANCE

This happened on the last Simhat Torah, in 1942. Only a handful of Jews had remained alive out of the five hundred thousand, formerly in the Polish capital.

Twenty Jews were gathered in the home of Rabbi Menahem Zemba, the last remaining rabbi in Warsaw, to observe Simhat Torah. Among them was Judah Leib Orlean, former director of the Beth Jacob Teachers' Seminary, who had devoted his life to religious education. At the proper time they brought forth the scrolls of the Torah; and, sorrowfully reciting the verses, which in former years had been joyously chanted, they wearily plodded the *hakafot* about the table.

Suddenly a boy of twelve appeared in the room. This was astonishing, for the Germans had already slain or deported, for extermination, all the Jewish children in the ghetto. Who could he be, and where had he come from? No one knew.

Orlean ran to the boy, and embracing him together with his Torah, cried out, "Young Jew with the holy Torah!" He swept him along in an exultant *hassidic* dance. The others joined the dance one by one, until all had formed a circle about the unknown boy, Orlean, and the Torah.

Bereaved fathers who had lost their entire families danced, with tears rolling down their faces, while the great educator reiterated, "Young Jew with the holy Torah! Young Jew with the holy Torah!"

This was the last dance of the last Jews on the last Simhat Torah in Warsaw.

(from Hillel Seidman's Diary)

HEBREW LETTERING

by Ludwig Yehuda

Wolpert, Jerusalem

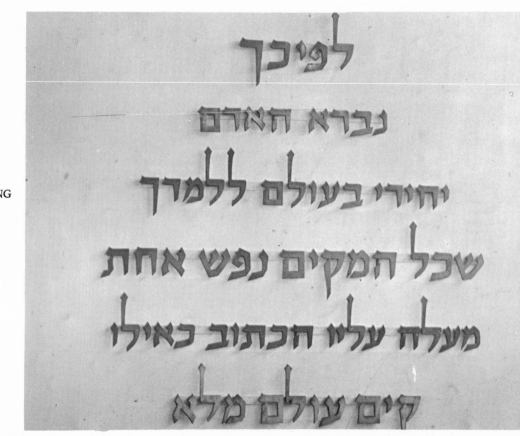

לפיכך

נברא האדם

יחידי בעולם ללמדך

שכל המקים נפש אחת

מעלה עליו הכתוב כאילו

קים עולם מלא

Therefore, but a single man was created in the world, to teach that if any man has caused a single soul to perish from the world, Scripture imputes it to him as though he has caused a whole world to perish; and if man saves alive a single soul from the world, Scripture imputes it to him as though he had saved alive a whole world . . . Maimonides

אֲנִי מַאֲמִין בֶּאֱמוּנָה שְׁלֵמָה בְּבִיאַת הַמָּשִׁיחַ:
וְאַף עַל פִּי שֶׁיִּתְמַהְמֵהַּ, עִם כָּל זֶה אֲנִי מַאֲמִין !

"I BELIEVE WITH PERFECT FAITH IN THE COMING OF THE MES-
SIAH; AND THOUGH HE TARRY, NONE THE LESS DO I BELIEVE.

"THE WAYFARER DREAMS OF THE COMING OF THE MESSIAH"
Painting by Elias Newman, New York City
Collection: Brandeis University, Waltham, Mass.

87

TU BI'SHEVAT

There is a special New Year for trees in the Jewish calendar. It is called *Hamishah Asar bi'Shevat,* sometimes *Tu bi'Shevat,* because the letters spelling *Tu* have the numerical value of fifteen. The middle of the fifth Jewish month *Shevat,* coming some weeks before the United States has its spring, generally marks the end of Israel's rainy season. The sap becomes active in the trees, and they attain new life and growth.

There is no mention of such a festival in the Bible. Its value was in the fact that it marked the beginning of a new agricultural year in the Holy Land. One tenth — a tithe — of all produce was taken as tax for the Temple and government; since one was not permitted to pay the tithes of one year with produce of another year, it was necessary to set a time for demarcation. This was the beginning of springtime in the Holy Land. With great exultation new trees were planted everywhere. In the Talmud we are told of the custom of planting a cedar sapling for a boy baby, and a cypress for a girl. When they grew up, poles from these trees would be used to hold up their wedding canopies.

BOYS PLANTING SAPLINGS, ISRAEL
Courtesy, Jewish National Fund, New York

In addition to planting, the people celebrate by eating a great variey of fruits on that day. There is song and music and parties for children. Although *Hamishah Asar bi-Shevat* was always considered a semi-festival, in today's Israel it has taken on the character of a national celebration, observed and honored by old and young.

.. **"Thou shall not destroy the trees ... for the tree of the field is man's life."**

CHILDREN IN THE CITIES OBSERVE THE HOLIDAY FOR PLANTING (ISRAEL)
Courtesy, Zionist Archives and Library, New York City

"It is forbidden to dwell in a city that has no garden in it." *Talmud Yerushalmi*

" . . . And when ye shall come into the land
and shall have planted all manner of trees . . ."
Lev. 19:23

"THE GREATNESS OF MORDECAI" Drawing by Lucas Van der Leyden, Dutch, early 16th century
Courtesy, The Metropolitan Museum of Art, New York City

PURIM

One of the happiest days in the calendar of the Jews is the *Purim* festival, the 14th of *Adar,* whose origin is narrated in the biblical Book of Esther. The deliverance of Persian Jewry from a plot by a highplaced official to exterminate them all, has given the name *Purim* to a great number of local celebrations of days wherein small communities were saved from destruction by some extraordinary event.

But *Purim* itself means "lots," the casting of lots. The emperor of the hundred and twenty-seven provinces of the mighty Persian Empire, Ahasuerus (perhaps Artaxerxes, as we know the name in history), had appointed one Haman as his prime minister. Haman, irked because a certain leading Jew, Mordecai, who worshiped only the God of Israel, would not bow down to him at the king's gate, had the king sign a decree to wipe out all the Jews in the empire. The date for extermination was chosen by lot.

As unusual procession of incidents stayed execution of the decree, brought about the death of Haman and his equally cruel sons, and elevated Mordecai to Haman's high office. For Ahasuerus had sent away his former queen, Vashti, and his chamberlains had spent a year choosing the handsomest lass in Persia as the new queen. This was Esther, who for reasons of security did not at first divulge her origin or Mordecai's until it became necessary to save her people from destruction. Then, on Mordecai's prompting — "Think not . . . that thou shalt escape . . . more than all the Jews . . . and who knoweth whether thou are not come to royal estate

90

" . . . and that these days of Purim should not fail from among the Jews, nor the memorial of them perish from their seed." *Esther 9:28*

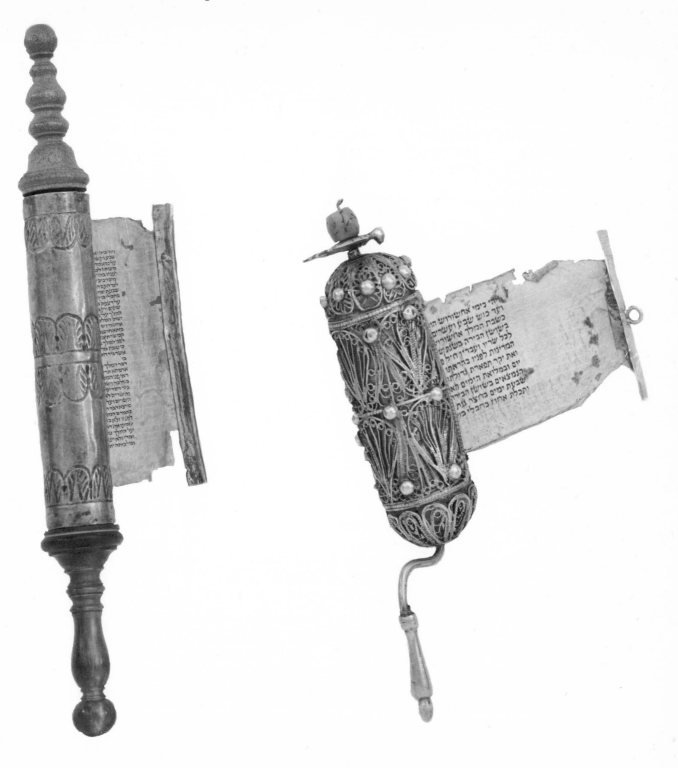

SCROLLS OF ESTHER (MEGILLOTH)
Left: Silver case, Galicia, early 19th century
Right: Silver filigree, Eastern Europe, 18th century

for such a time as this?"—she exposed Haman, the decree was overcome by another permitting the Jews to slay their assailants, and the Jews were accorded new life and honor.

The day before *Purim*, Adar 13, is a fast day, for thereon did Esther and her people fast before the Lord, to avert the evil decree. At evening and morning services the entire scroll of Esther *(Megillah)* is chanted while noisy children grow wild at every mention of Haman's name. They twirl noisemakers, shout, and stamp, and not infrequently go completely out of control. Everyone has a good time, whether youth or adult. Most Jewish schools conduct Purim plays and entertainment. And there is always the Purim *seudah* (feast) to conclude the festival.

The finest observance of the holiday, however, is the custom of sending food to friends and the poor *(mishloah manot)*. For thus did our ancestors also celebrate the day — since Jews have always indicated their joyful emotions by giving to charity and bringing light into darkened lives.

The day after *Purim* is called *Shushan Purim*. This is so named because the Jews of Shushan, the capital, were kept busy fighting off their enemies for an additional day.

Many other "Purims" established for later acts of deliverance are observed in Tiberias of Israel, in Egypt, Frankfort, Saragosa, and numerous other places. It is therefore quite correct for a people that has been persecuted in so many times and regions to repeat the dictum of Israel's sages: "While all the other festivals may be annulled, Purim will never disappear."

AMERICAN CHILDREN STAGING A PURIM PLAY
Courtesy, Ramaz School, New York City
"The Jews had light and gladness, and joy and honor." *Esther 8:16*

PESAH

SILVER CANDLESTICK FOR BURNING LEAVEN ON THE EVENING
BEFORE THE PASSOVER SEDER, by Ilya Schor, New York City.
Courtesy, Siegfried Bendheim, New York City
"All manner of leaven that is in my possession, which I have not seen or
removed, shall be considered null and void, and accounted as the dust of the
earth" (recited after the search for leaven).

PASSOVER PLATE, Italy, 1614
Faience. Biblical scenes: Joseph revealing himself to his brothers, Israelites at *seder* in Egypt, and figures of Moses, Aaron, David, and Solomon. Inscription is the text of the *kiddush* and the order of the *seder*
Courtesy, The Jewish Museum, New York City

Passover, which falls on the fifteenth of *Nissan,* the period of Israel's deliverance from Egyptian bondage, became one of the three pilgrimage festivals, when every Israelite, or his representative, went up to sacrifice at the Temple in Jerusalem. The others are *Sukkot* and *Shavuot.*

For each of these festivals marks a great day in Jewish history, while also serving as an agricultural landmark. *Sukkot* is the time for ingathering of the fruit; Passover for the early harvest, and *Shavuot* the second harvest. Each has special readings from the Bible, as well as observances applying to planting and reaping on the sacred soil.

The biblical story of Israel's liberation from their long slavery in Egypt is universally known. At first Joseph and his brethren, their families and descend-

ants, prospered in that land. Then arose a new Pharaoh who feared lest the Israelites "grow too mighty, join Egypt's enemies," and threaten his power. He en-
slaved the entire people, forcing them to perform the most difficult labor. Since
they still kept growing in numbers, he decreed that all Jewish boy babies be slaughtered. But the infant Moses was saved, grew up in the palace of Pharaoh's daughter, and when the time came recognized his origin and led the redemption of
his people.

But Passover as a festival of human freedom is also related to the event at
Mount Sinai. The Hebrews were not delivered from Egyptian bondage only that
they might achieve political liberty, national independence. They were sent forth
in order "that they might serve the Lord." Hence the Exodus was complete

MODEL SEDER FOR CHILDREN OF AN AMERICAN JEWISH SCHOOL
Courtesy, Ramaz School, New York City

WINE CUP FOR PROPHET ELIJAH
Silver, repousee work and cast
In addition to the traditional four cups of wine drunk during the *seder,* a special cup is filled with wine for the prophet Elijah, who will announce the coming of the Messiah.
Courtesy, The Jewish Museum, New York City

only when the Israelites reached Mount Sinai, and there learnt how to conduct themselves in relation to both God and man. Physical freedom alone is not sufficient; as one rabbi expressed it, "There is no free man except him who engages in the Torah." Freedom must be accompanied by law, so that men may be able best to live together. Not the mere deliverance of human beings from slavery made Israel a nation, but the giving of the Law at the festival time known as *Shavuot.*

The story of Passover has given inspiration to countless millions through the centuries, to break the bonds of slavery and lift their heads to the level of any man. Its influence can be traced in the liberation movements of France, America, and many other peoples that revolted to freedom. For independence is the first requisite in the proper development of humanity.

As the late Chief Rabbi Joseph H. Hertz of the British Empire expressed the thought in his Daily Prayer Book: "Passover . . commemorates an event — the redemption of Israel from Egyptian slavery—that has changed the destinies of humanity. The story of that event . . has become one of the parables of mankind; and has been a light to the Western peoples in their long and weary warfare for liberty. It taught them that God, Who in Egypt espoused the cause of brick-making slaves

PAGES FROM THE PASSOVER HAGGADAH, painted by Aaron Herlingen of Gewitsch (Moravia), 18th century. From the collections of the Bezalel Museum, Jerusalem
Courtesy, American Fund for Israel Institutions

97

against a royal oppressor, was a God of justice and freedom . . . . Thus, the most Jewish of the festivals, Israel's birthday, is as timely today as it was thousands of years ago, and has a message for men of all creeds and all races."

After a long stay away from Egypt, during which time he married the daughter of a priest of neighboring Midian and had two sons, Moses returned with his brother Aaron—to the court of Pharaoh. Pharaoh was persuaded, by way of miracles, to release his slaves, but quickly changed his mind. It took ten plagues, particularly the last, which brought about the death of all firstborn sons among the Egyptians, to assure his final consent. Even then, he sent his army after the fleeing slaves, and the soldiers drowned in the Red Sea — which had first divided to permit the Israelites to cross.

The people were unable to prepare their dough properly in escaping. The unleavened bread which they baked in the sun as they traveled is the *matzah* which the Bible compels us to eat in place of ordinary bread through all the days of the festival. The holiday is therefore known as *Hag ha-Matzot,* Feast of Unleavened Bread.

Passover observance really begins on the morning before the holiday. For all

Pages from Hagaddah, Central European, 15th century. Showing the hard labor of the Israelites in Egypt in building the two cities, Pithom and Raamses.

firstborn sons are expected to fast on that day, to memorialize the escape of the Jewish firstborn sons when the Angel of Death entered the homes of the Egyptians during the final plague. To avoid this requirement, present day oldest sons meet after morning service, and complete some sacred book, thus making the day a festive one, on which no fast may be observed.

The dietary laws are most strict in regard to Passover. The slightest amount of leaven, or souring stuff *(hametz)*, is prohibited in the home. On the previous eve, before the holiday begins, we search in all the crannies of the house for bits of this *hametz*, and it is all burnt the following morning, with suitable blessings and formulas. The greatest care is taken to purchase only food prepared according to the Passover laws. Virtually all dishes, pots, and utensils are different, and these are used on Passover only.

The great celebration of the festival is the *seder,* for the first two nights (one night only, of course, in Israel), when the *Haggadah* (narration) of Passover is read, special foods are blessed and eaten, and a veritable banquet is served. Even the least observant of adult Jews looks back upon the *seder* as the happiest occasion of life with his parents.

Outside Israel (because of the time difference) there are two days of full observance, four of partial observance *(Hol ha-Moed),* and two more days of full festival. In Israel there are seven days in all, only the first and last of which are fully observed. On Passover, the rainy season having ended, there is a special prayer for dew. On the second night begins the counting of the Omer, the ancient measure of the winter barley offered in the Temple. This counting proceeds for forty-nine days, and culminates in the festival of *Shavuot.*

Another name for Passover is *Hag he-Aviv,* Spring Festival. It is a season of rebirth, with nature coming to life again, and the light of liberty and life spreading over the peoples. It has always been a festival of hope and gratitude for all mankind.

PASSOVER PLATE, Poland, 17th century
Brass; rampant lions support medallion inscribed, "Thus did Hillel at the time the Temple existed," from the Haggadah.

100

OMER CALENDAR IN FORM OF TORAH ARK, Holland, 18th century
Wooden case holding parchment manuscript with painted floral decorations
Omer scroll used in some synagogues for counting the 49 days between the second day of Passover and
Shavuot. "And ye shall count unto you from the morrow after the day of rest, from the day that ye
brought the sheaf of the waving; seven weeks shall there be complete; even unto the morrow after the
seventh week shall ye number fifty days." *Lev. 23:15, 16*
Courtesy, The Jewish Museum, New York City

LAG BA'OMER

The counting of the *Omer* (a measure of barley), which comprises the days between Passover and Shavuot, is one of mourning and sad memories. No feasts,
no weddings, may then be celebrated.

But the thirty-third day of this period, known as *Lag ba-Omer* (the letters
"L-g" have the Hebrew numerical value of thirty-three) is an exception. This day
is linked with three distinguished names in Jewish history—Bar Kochba, who led

101

"SAFED IN GALILEE" water color by Elias Newman
The wonderful landscape renders it the fit homeland of the lofty thoughts of poets and visionaries, and the "precious enclave" of mysticism, Kabbalah, and Hassidism.
Courtesy, Dr. Israel Goldstein, New York City.

the revolt against the Romans eighteen centuries ago, Rabbi Akiba, and Rabbi Simeon bar Yochai. For three years Bar Kochba fought on, until overwhelmed by the Roman legions. Rabbi Akiba, one of the greatest of talmudic scholars, though all of ninety years old, fought with him, as did his forty thousand disciples. A mysterious plague destroyed twenty-four thousand of these embattled students; it was lifted on the thirty-third day of the *Omer*. Rabbi Simeon, forbidden to teach the Torah, is said to have hidden in a cave for many years; on *Lag ba-Omer* he revealed to his students many secrets of the Torah.

It has been the custom for children to cease their studies on the day, and betake themselves to the open fields, in memory of these ancient events. In Israel today many make a pilgrimage to Meron, a village in Galilee, where Rabbi Simeon is buried. At midnight they kindle a bonfire and dance until dawn. The idea of bonfires and dances has spread, and now similar celebrations take place throughout the land.

SHAVUOT

TORAH CROWN, Poland, 1778
Silver, hammered, with bird finial
Courtesy, The Jewish Museum, New York City

Hag ha-shavuot means the Feast of Weeks. It takes place seven weeks after the counting of the *Omer* begins on Passover. It is one of the pilgrimage festivals; and on it *bikkurim*, or first fruits, are brought to the Temple. It is also *Hag ha-Katzir*, Feast of the Harvest (wheat). That is why the synagogues today are so beautifully decorated with flowers and fruit on the holiday. *Shavuot* falls on the sixth of *Sivan*, in May or early June.

But it is primarily remembered as *Zeman Mattan Toratenu*—the Time of the Giving of Our Law. For on this day according to tradition the Torah was submitted to Israel from Mount Sinai through Moses. *Shavuot* is therefore the birthday of the Jewish religion, as Passover is the birthday of the Jewish nation.

Milk foods and honey are largely eaten on *Shavuot*. This custom is derived from the phrase in the Song of Songs, "Honey and milk shall be under your tongue" —an implication, say the sages, that the words of the Torah may be as pleasant and acceptable to our ears and hearts as are milk and honey to our tongues.

Because of its relationship to the Torah, *Shavuot* has long been an acceptable time for a child to begin his religious studies. Many men spend the entire first night in studying *Tikkun Shavuot*. The latter is an anthology from the Bible, Talmud, the mystic Zohar, and many other sacred volumes. A long poem by Rabbi Meir ben Isaac of Orleans, who lived in the eleventh century, is recited with a special chant before the synagogue reading from the Torah during the morning services; this poem, called *Akdamut*, praises the Jewish people for their attachment to their Creator and to His Law.

The special reading for *Shavuot* is the Book of Ruth. For in telling the story of this ancestor of King David, and her acceptance of Israel's religion, the Bible gives an account of the grain harvest, and of how the poor were aided during the reaping. There is also a tradition, found in the Talmud, that David was born and died on *Shavuot*.

On Passover we are commanded to assume that we ourselves are participating in the Exodus from Egypt and are being freed from bondage. On *Shavuot* it is brought home to us that the Torah given on Mount Sinai was also given to us; we accept it anew and once again dedicate ourselves to its glorious teachings.

"FEAST OF WEEKS" (SHAVUOT) by Moritz Oppenheim (1880-1882), Germany
"And thou shalt keep the feast of weeks unto the Lord thy God . . . and thou shalt rejoice before the
Lord thy God . . ." *Deut. 16:10, 11*
Courtesy, Oscar Gruss, New York City

"How were the first fruits brought? Those who lived near Jerusalem brought fresh figs and grapes, and those who lived far away brought dried figs and raisins. In front of them went an ox, its horns overlaid with gold and a wreath of olive leaves on its head.

"The flute played before them until they reached Jerusalem. They then sent messengers and decorated their first fruits. The rulers, the chief priests, and the treasurers of the Temple went out to meet them; and all the craftsmen of Jerusalem stood up and greeted them with the words, 'Brethren, ye are welcome!' (Talmud)

And when ye reap the harvest of your land, thou shalt not wholly reap the corner of thy field . . . .
And thou shalt not glean thy vineyard . . . Thou shalt leave them for the poor and for the strangers . . . .   Lev. 19:9-10

"RUTH" by E. M. Lilien, (1874-1925)
"And she gleaned in the field after the reapers"

בִּימֵי שְׁפֹט הַשֹּׁפְטִים וַיְהִי רָעָב בָּאָרֶץ וַיֵּלֶךְ

אִישׁ מִבֵּית לֶחֶם יְהוּדָה לָגוּר בִּשְׂדֵי מוֹאָב הוּא

אִשְׁתּוֹ וּשְׁנֵי בָנָיו: וְשֵׁם הָאִישׁ אֱלִימֶלֶךְ וְשֵׁם אִשְׁתּוֹ נָעֳמִי וְשֵׁם

שְׁנֵי בָנָיו מַחְלוֹן וְכִלְיוֹן אֶפְרָתִים מִבֵּית לֶחֶם יְהוּדָה וַיָּבֹאוּ שְׂדֵי

מוֹאָב וַיִּהְיוּ שָׁם: וַיָּמָת אֱלִימֶלֶךְ אִישׁ נָעֳמִי וַתִּשָּׁאֵר הִיא וּשְׁנֵי

בָנֶיהָ: וַיִּשְׂאוּ לָהֶם נָשִׁים מֹאֲבִיּוֹת שֵׁם הָאַחַת עָרְפָּה וְשֵׁם

THE WRITTEN LAW

A Bible Published by the Jerusalem Bible Publishing Company

BIBLE — TANAKH
The Hebrew Bible consists of twenty-four books grouped into three divisions: (a) *Torah* — the Law or Five Books of Moses; (b) *Nebiim* — the Prophets; and (c) *Ketubim* — Hagiographa or Holy Writings. From the initial letters of the Hebrew names for the three divisions we get the commonly used word for the Bible, *Tanakh.*

"And these words, which I command thee this day, shall be upon thy heart; and thou shalt teach them diligently unto thy children . . . . "
Deut. 6:6-7

This book of the law shall not depart out of thy mouth, but thou shalt meditate therein day and night, that thou mayest observe to do according to all that is written therein; for then thou shalt make thy ways prosperous, and then thou shalt have good success.
Josh. 1:8

108

THE ORAL LAW

מאימתי

מאימתי קורין את שמע בערבין. משעה שהכהנים נכנסים לאכול בתרומתן. כהנים שנטמאו וטבלו והעריב שמשן והגיע עתם לאכול בתרומתן...

קורין את שמע בערבין א משעה שהכהנים
נכנסים לאכול בתרומתן עד סוף האשמורה
הראשונה דברי רבי אליעזר וחכמים אומרים
עד חצות רבן גמליאל אומר ג עד שיעלה
עמוד השחר מעשה ובאו בניו מבית המשתה
אמרו לו לא קרינו את שמע אמר להם אם לא
עלה עמוד השחר חייבין אתם לקרות ולא זו
בלבד אמרו אלא א כל מה שאמרו חכמים
עד חצות מצותן עד שיעלה עמוד השחר
ב ה הקטר חלבים ואברים מצותן עד שיעלה
עמוד השחר ג ה וכל הנאכלים ליום אחד
מצותן עד שיעלה עמוד השחר אם כן למה
אמרו חכמים עד חצות כדי להרחיק אדם מן
העבירה : גמ' ז תנא היכא קאי דקתני מאימתי
ותו מאי שנא דתני בערבית ברישא לתני
דשחרית ברישא תנא אקרא קאי ה דכתיב
ובקומך והכי קתני זמן קריאת שמע
דשכיבה אימת משעה שהכהנים נכנסין לאכול
בתרומתן ואי בעית אימא יליף מברייתו של
עולם דכתיב °ויהי ערב ויהי בקר יום אחד אי
הכי סיפא ° דקתני ' ובשחר מברך שתים
לפניה ואחת לאחריה ובערב מברך שתי לפניה
ושתי ' לאחריה לתני דערבית ברישא תנא פתח
בערבית והדר תני בשחרית עד דקאי בשחרית
פריש מילי דשחרית והדר פריש מילי דערבית:
אמר מר משעה שהכהנים נכנסים לאכול בתרומתן
מכדי כהנים אימת קא אכלי תרומה משעת צאת
הכוכבים לתני משעת צאת הכוכבים מלתא אגב
אורחיה קמשמע לן ז כהנים אימת קא אכלי
בתרומה משעת צאת הכוכבי' והא קמ"ל דכפרה לא מעכבא כדתניא ח ובאיק °
השמש וטהר ז ביאת שמשו מעכבתו מלאכול בתרומה ואין כפרתו מעכבתו בכ
מלאכול בתרומה ט וממאי דהאי ובא השמש ביאת השמש והאי וטהר מהר יומא
דילמא

FIRST PAGE OF THE FIRST VOLUME OF THE TALMUD, CALLED BERAKHOT

Center text: The Mishnah and Gemara, the code of Jewish law and rabbinic discussions thereof. Surrounding text: Commentaries of *Rashi* (1040-1105), the *Tosaphot,* and others.

"THE WAILING WALL" oil by D. Bida
"How doth the city sit solitary, that was full of people . . . from the daughter of Zion all her beauty is departed." *Lamentations*
Courtesy, The Jewish Museum, New York City

TISHAH B'AV

Tishah B'Av, the ninth day of the month Av (or Ab), is an extraordinary date in Jewish history.

On that day, says the Talmud, occurred these fearful events: "The decree that Israel should wander through the wilderness for forty years; the destruction of the First Temple by Nebuchadnezzar (586 before the common era), and of the Second Temple by Titus (in the year 70); fall of the fortress of Bethar (135); the subsequent defeat of Bar Kochba and massacre of his men; and the plowing up of Jerusalem (under Hadrian, 135)."

110

But there were later calamities on the ninth of Av. It was on this day, in 1290, that Edward I signed the edict expelling the Jews from England; and in 1492, 300,000 Jews, led by Abarbanel, began their departure from the Spain of Ferdinand and Isabella. The Jews of Spain had lived there in peace for centuries, and enriched the country materially as well as in literature and scholarship. They could no longer endure the fear and tortures of the Inquisition. Most of them were expelled, perished from hunger, drowned, or were sold into slavery.

To our sages, the greatest of all calamities was that which first sent the Jewish people into exile. To mourn the destruction of the temples, Jews were commanded to abstain from food and labor on the ninth of Av. It is said that all who thus mourn for Jerusalem will witness the restoration of its ancient glory — which seems to mean that only by mourning our loss through the ages, and commemorating our past greatness, could we hope to seek to retrieve the Holy City of our past. This prophecy is being realized today, through the merit of those who for so long fasted and wept on the day of destruction. Recall of the past has been the major factor in recognizing our unity, our continuity, and our destiny.

Prayer shawl and phylacteries are not worn at early services, to show our mourning. Instead they are donned for the afternoon prayer. In announcing the coming of the Hebrew month we call it *Menahem Av,* "menahem" meaning comforter. Hope has sprung eternally among the exiled people of Israel.

Observant Jews doff their shoes and seat themselves on the floor when they begin the services in the synagogue. The Lamentations of Jeremiah are mournfully chanted, both in the evening and the morning, generally by dim lights. *Ekhah,* Hebrew name of Lamentations, is the first word of the book. No sadder elegy has ever been written. *Kinnot,* dirges, are recited through the day. Yet in all of these, particularly the odes composed by Judah Halevi, the hope of a restored Zion is never lacking.

MODEL OF KING SOLOMON'S TEMPLE, built by Joseph Doctorowitz.
Based on text from the Bible.
Courtesy, The Jewish Museum, New York City

SPECIAL CEREMONY ON TISHAH B'AV IN KING DAVID'S TOMB ON MT. ZION, JERUSALEM
Crowns are removed from their resting place for this day of mourning.
Courtesy, New York University J.C.F. Library of Judaica.

For it has been the immemorial tradition in Jewry that at the very moment God punishes His people he prepares for their healing. Our ancestors believed that on the day the Temple was destroyed occurred the birth of the Messiah. And each year, on the Sabbath following Tishah B'Av — called *Shabbat Nahamu* — we read the fortieth chapter of Isaiah, one of the most beautiful visions in all literature:

> Comfort ye, comfort ye, My people,
> Saith your God.
> Bid Jerusalem take heart,
> And proclaim unto her,
> That her time of service is accomplished,
> That her guilt is paid off;
> That she hath received of the Lord's hand
> Double for all her sins.

112

"DESTRUCTION OF JERUSALEM" oil by Bernard Picart (1712)

LAMENTATIONS

How doth the city sit solitary,
That was full of people!
How is she become as a widow!
She that was great among the nations,
And princess among the provinces,
How is she become tributary!
She weepeth sore in the night,
And her tears are on her cheeks;
She hath none to comfort her
Among all her lovers;
All her friends have dealt treacherously with her,
They are become her enemies.

Lam. 1: 1-2

The ways of Zion do mourn,
Because none come to the solemn assembly;
All her gates are desolate,
Her priests sigh;
Her virgins are afflicted,
And she herself is in bitterness.

Lam. 1: 4

And gone is from the daughter of Zion
All her splendour;
Her princes are become like harts
That find no pasture,
And they are gone without strength
Before the pursuer.
Jerusalem remembereth
In the days of her affliction and of her anguish
All her treasures that she had
From the days of old;
Now that her people fall by the hand of the adversary,
And none doth help her,
The adversaries have seen her,
They have mocked at her desolations.

Lam. 1: 6-7

For these things I weep;
Mine eye, mine eye runneth down with water;
Because the comforter is far from me,
Even he that should refresh my soul;
My children are desolate,
Because the enemy hath prevailed.

Lam. 1: 16

I called for my lovers,
But they deceived me;
My priests and mine elders
Perished in the city,
While they sought them food
To refresh their souls.
Behold, O Lord, for I am in distress,
Mine inwards burn;
My heart is turned within me,
For I have grievously rebelled.
Abroad the sword bereaveth,
At home there is the like of death.

Lam. 1: 19-20

Arise, cry out in the night,
At the beginning of the watches;
Pour out thy heart like water
Before the face of the Lord;
Lift up thy hands toward Him
For the life of thy young children,
That faint for hunger
At the head of every street.

Lam. 2: 19

"JEREMIAH," by E. M. Lilien (1874-1925)

I am the man that hath seen affliction
By the rod of His wrath.
He hath led me and caused me to walk
In darkness and not in light.

Lam. 3: 1-2

How is the gold become dim!
How is the most fine gold changed!
The hallowed stones are poured out
At the head of every street!
The precious sons of Zion,
Comparable to fine gold,
How are they esteemed as earthen pitchers,
The work of the hands of the potter!
Even the jackals draw out the breast,
They give suck to their young ones;
The daughter of my people is become cruel,
Like the ostriches in the wilderness.

Lam. 4: 1-3

Remember, O Lord, what is come upon us;
Behold, and see our reproach.
Our inheritance is turned unto strangers,
Our houses unto aliens.
We are become orphans and fatherless,
Our mothers are as widows.
We have drunk our water for money;
Our wood cometh to us for price.
To our very necks we are pursued;
We labour, and have no rest.

Lam. 5: 1-5

Turn thou us unto Thee, O Lord,
   and we shall be turned;
Renew our days as of old.

Lam. 5: 21

Menorah designed at New Bezalel Arts and Crafts School, Jerusalem
Courtesy, American Fund for Israel Institutions.

OTHER FASTS

There are also other fast days in Judaism, observed from sunrise rather than from the previous evening, as is the case with *Yom Kippur* and *Tish'ah B'Av*. Some pious Jews, in search of repentance, fast a cycle of Monday, Thursday, and Monday, after Passover or *Sukkot*. Fasts as a means of beseeching God for help and victory, are frequently mentioned in the Bible. Communities have often fasted in times of distress. During the Hitler persecutions rabbis throughout the world also ordained fasts of supplication.

On the seventeenth of *Tammuz* the walls of Jerusalem were breached, leading to destruction of the Second Temple in 70 A.D. The Talmud records other misfortunes that took place on that day, such as: the tablets of the Ten Commandments were broken; and the daily Temple offerings ceased during the siege of Jerusalem, for lack of animals. Three weeks after the seventeenth of *Tammuz* is the ninth of Av, when the first destruction took place.

There is also *Tzom Gedaliah,* the fast decreed for the day after *Rosh Ha-shanah* because of the murder on that day of Gedaliah, governor appointed by Nebuchadnezzar, which brought fearful retaliation upon the people. Another fast falls on the tenth of *Tevet,* when Nebuchadnezzar began his siege.

But it must be remembered that on the whole, despite all these evidences, Judaism does not favor excess of self-mortification.

115

THE SYNAGOGUE

For nearly twenty-five hundred years the synagogue has been the fortress of the Jewish spirit. When the First Temple was destroyed in 586 B.C.E., and our forefathers were exiled to Babylonia, they would gather there to read passages from the Torah and the Prophets, to recall the Temple ceremonies, and to observe the fast and feast days. These meetings were called *knesset,* gathering. First they met in private homes. When they erected permanent houses of worship, each became a *Bet Knesset* — house of meeting. The Greek word *synagogue* has the same meaning.

The Jews who returned from Babylonian exile in 536 B.C.E. rebuilt the Temple. But everywhere outside the Land they continued building synagogues. Philo, first century phil-

INTERIOR OF PORTUGUESE SYNAGOGUE, AMSTERDAM. Dedicated 1675.

RUINS OF ANCIENT SYNAGOGUE AT KFAR BIRAM

BETH ALPHA SYNAGOGUE, part of the large mosaic floor from this 6th century synagogue, discovered when Jewish pioneer settlers were digging trenches for foundation walls of a new building.

osopher of Alexandria, Egypt, wrote: "On the seventh day the Jews stop all work and proceed to sacred spots which they call synagogues. There, arranged in rows according to their ages, the younger below the older, they sit quietly as befits the occasion, with attentive ears. Then one of them takes the book, and reads aloud to the others . . . "

After destruction of the Second Temple in the year 70, the synagogue acquired many new functions. It became both house of worship, center of study, and focal point for the community. Here religious leaders addressed the people; wayfarers came for help and hospitality; and emissaries from the Holy Land or other communities sought assistance. In addition to *Bet Knesset,* the synagogue was called *Bet Am,* house of the people; *Bet Tefillah,* house of prayer; and *Bet Midrash,* house of study.

In countries of oppression, building synagogues was often prohibited, or their height was kept below that of churches or mosques. But in ancient Alexandria the synagogue was large and imposing. Excavations in Syria and Palestine have uncovered remains of richly adorned Jewish houses of worship in Dura Europe, Capernaum, Beth Alpha, and many other sites.

Despite a great variety of arch-

TORAH ARK IN THE SYNAGOGUE OF ARI, OLDEST SYNAGOGUE IN SAFED, ISRAEL

"SYNAGOGUE OF VILNA, POLAND" by Marc Chagall
Courtesy, M. Cottin, Lakewood, New Jersey

itecture, synagogue buildings have clung to certain rules in construction. The most important feature has always been the Holy Ark, or *Aron ha-kodesh,* set in a wall recess to face the congregation. This permanent receptacle for the Scrolls of the Law is named after the *Aron ha-Berit,* or Ark of the Convenant, which held the Ten Commandments when the early Israelites traversed the desert. As a rule the Ark is built in the east wall, so that the worshipers may face east as they pray.

Above the Ark there are representations of the Tables of the Law, and other decorations, such as rampant lions of Judah. As the children of Israel, in their wanderings,

INTERIOR OF SYNAGOGUE HURVAH
One of the oldest synagogues in Old
Jerusalem, destroyed by the Arabs in 1948

hung a curtain before the Ark, synagogues today employ the highly ornate, embroidered *parokhet,* made of satin or velvet, to embellish their own Arks. There may be a short hanging also, called *kapporet,* emulating the long descriptions of the sacred object in the Book of Exodus.

The *Ner Tamid,* Eternal Light, gleams perpetually before every synagogue Ark. It is a symbol of God's presence among His creatures. In Temple days the lamp that was never extinguished was fed with pure olive oil. Today electric bulbs serve the same purpose in most American synagogues.

The *bimah,* or reading platform, where the assigned portions from the Torah and the Prophets are recited, is an elevated structure found just before the Ark. In all Sephardic structures, and most Ashkenazic synagogues completely traditional, the *bimah* is placed in the center of the house of worship. This is reminiscent of the middle compartment of the Temple, where in ancient days stood altar, table, and candelabrum.

121

INTERIOR VIEW OF MODERN YESHURUN SYNAGOGUE IN JERUSALEM, showing the platform
and the Torah Ark

The large seven-branched candelabrum, as prescribed by Exodus, is found in many
fine metals and designs in all congregations. The reading desk is covered by embroidered fabrics. It has been the custom for Jews to donate the several articles of fur-
niture and their coverings in honor of deceased relatives; thus they may bear not alone
sacred inscriptions, but also the names of those memorialized.

The synagogue has always been used for discourses by the spiritual leader or a
visiting preacher as well as for prayer. The prayers were varied as to content and
phraseology, and in early centuries full freedom for such variations was permitted readers and worshipers. In the ninth century, Rab Amram for the first time — so far as
extant manuscripts show — established a permanent order of prayers. Since that
time prayerbooks for every day, the Sabbath, and the festivals, as well as the high
holidays, have been produced, until in these days there are standard liturgies
for all purposes, published in many forms but all based upon the accepted prayers and
blessings employed for many generations.

It must never be forgotten that the synagogue was at no time a mere meeting
place for prayer quorums (*minyanim*). Judaism did not, and does not, look upon

TOURO SYNAGOGUE, Newport, Rhode Island
The oldest synagogue building in the United States, dedicated in 1763 (congregation founded 1658)

repetition of prescribed orisons as its sole purpose. It has always been the school house (the common word "schul" applied to traditional synagogues is really the German word for school). Also it has served as Bet *haMidrash,* the academy for more advanced students, and for mature men who wish to study Talmud and other sacred volumes between services or at other available seasons.

Special service in 1954 at Manhattan's Congregation Shearith Israel, oldest Jewish congregation in the United States, inaugurating the celebration of the anniversary of three hundred years of American Jewish life. Courtesy, Congregation Shearith Israel, New York City

In the synagogue too, weddings were celebrated; and from it funerals of important and learned men were conducted. Public announcements of importance were made from the *bimah;* it was permitted on Sabbath for petitioners seeking redress from wrongs to interrupt the reading service to address the congregation. When rabbinical courts sought to enforce their decrees, they did so through the forum afforded by the synagogue platform.

The *schul* has perennially served as the center of philanthropy. A poor box was suspended near the door, for all to see. From its receipts local poor and indigent transients were cared for. There was a charity chest *(kuppah)* to provide a fuller quota of funds to assist the town charities. In many towns travelers slept in the synagogue, and ate their Sabbath meal there. For this reason there developed the custom of reciting the *kiddush* at synagogue services, for the benefit of strangers who would not hear this benediction at home. On Passover, when strangers are brought into the homes of local householders, the *kiddush* is not recited in the holy place.

A notable recent occurrence in America is the dynamic interest in the construction of synagogues and temples, with much care and attention focused on architectural design and beauty of ornamentation. Following are examples of modern design applied to houses of worship representing orthodox, conservative, and reform Judaism.

TAYLOR ROAD SYNAGOGUE, CLEVELAND HEIGHTS, OHIO. (ORTHODOX)

Milo S. Holdstein, A.I.A., Architect
Albert Strom, Interior Design

CONGREGATION ADATH JESHURUN (CONSERVATIVE) ELKINS PARK, PA.

TEMPLE BETH-EL, PROVIDENCE, R. I. (REFORM)

Percival Goodman, Architect
Courtesy, Union of American Hebrew Congregations

"THE MIRACLE" by Jacques Lipchitz
Bronze
Courtesy, The Jewish Museum, New York City

EIGHT CLASSES OF CHARITY

Maimonides divided the dispensers of charity (*zedakah*) into eight classes according to rising degrees of merit:
1. Those who bestow charity but complainingly.
2. Those who do so cheerfully but give less than they should.
3. Those who contribute only when they are asked and the sum they are asked.
4. Those who give before they are requested to.
5. Those who give charity but do not know who benefits by it, although the recipient is aware from whom he has received it.
6. Those who give charity and do not disclose their names to those who have received it.
7. Those who do not know to whom their contribution will be given, while the recipients do not know from whom they have received it.
8. Those who extend a loan or bestow a gift upon the needy, or who take a poor man into partnership, or help him to establish himself in business, so that he should not be compelled to apply for charity. Such people practice the highest degree of charity.

BLESSING THE SABBATH CANDLES by Isidore Kaufmann
Courtesy, Oscar Gruss, New York City

For three and a half centuries pious Jewish women have pored over the pages of Tze-enah Ure-enah,* *a kind of household companion to the Five Books of Moses. Published by the Talmudist Jacob ben Isaac of Janow, Poland, in 1590, the book is a paraphrase in Old Yiddish of the Pentateuch (and the biblical portions reading during services), enriched by midrashic and other legends. These were intended for the edification of the common person, who had no access to the biblical commentaries in their original Hebrew sources. Since many members of the early audience for this popular work were illiterate, it was often read aloud to a company of women by a* lezerin, *or woman reader; the reading was accompanied by expressions of admiration, horror, sadness, or laughter, as the occasion demanded.*

Here is a typical selection from Tze-enah Ure-enah. *Can you see how entertaining it was to people who could not read the Bible in the original—and why it was a best seller for more than three centuries?*

*Literally, "Go forth and behold" from Song of Songs 3:11: "Go forth, O ye daughters of Zion, and behold King Solomon with the crown wherewith his mother crowned him in the day of his espousals, and in the day of the gladness of his heart."

129

"And Moses said unto the Lord, O my Lord, I am not eloquent, neither heretofore, nor since thou hast spoken unto thy servant; But I am slow of speech, and of a slow tongue."

For when Moses pulled the crown off Pharaoh's head as a babe, Pharaoh's astrologers said to him, We told you long ago that one would be born who would help the Israelites escape out of their exile—and this is he, certainly. Then Pharaoh set up a court of justice—Jethro, and Job, and Balaam. The one said, He is deserving of death. And the other said, He is still a child, with no intelligence. (And the third was silent.) They brought in one basin of gold and one of fire to see: If the child took the fire it would be known he had no intelligence as yet. But if he took the gold, he had intelligence, and should be killed. The child Moses reached to take the gold, but an angel came, and pushed him toward the fire. So Moses took a burning coal of fire, and put it in his mouth, and burned his tongue, and that is why he could not speak right.

"And the Lord said unto Moses in Midian, Go, return into Egypt, for all the men are dead which sought thy life" (Exodus 4:19).

God said to Moses, Go to Egypt, for Dathon and Abiram are dead who spoke against you to Pharaoh. Although they were still alive, He said they were dead because they had turned poor, which is like dying. And they would no longer be able to speak any slander against Moses, because their words would no longer be heard. So Moses took his wife and his children, and set them to riding on the ass that Abraham led Isaac to the Sacrifice on—and on that same ass the Messiah will ride when he comes.

"And afterward Moses and Aaron went in, and told Pharaoh, Thus saith the Lord God of Israel, Let my people go, that they may hold a feast unto me in the wilderness.

"And Pharaoh said, Who is the Lord, that I should obey his voice to let Israel go? I know not the Lord, neither will I let Israel go." (Exodus 5:1-2).

The Midrash says Pharaoh had a book containing the names of all the false gods. That is why he said, In my book the name of your God is not to be found. The author of *Bechaye* writes, Pharaoh was a great sage. He knew every king that reigned in every land, and he said, I do not know your God, because God had no land on the earth that he reigned over. But Pharaoh did not know that God reigns over the kings that reign in the world. Our sages have said: There is a parable of a priest who had a servant boy, a fool. And the priest went away. The servant boy runs to the graveyard, asking, Is my master here? Folks answer him, Indeed, your master is a priest, what would he be doing in the grave yard? The same way, Moses said to Pharaoh, You seek God among the gentiles, that are dead kings and have no dominion, but our God lives and he is king of kings. Then Pharaoh asked, What can your God do? Said Moses, He created heaven and earth, and all creatures, and makes rain to fall, and makes all things to grow, and raises up kings of the earth, and pulls down kings of the earth. Replied Pharaoh, I am the master of the world, I have created myself, and have created my river Nile. Said God to Moses, In as much as Pharaoh makes himself great with his river, you, Moses, shall make the water of the river Nile to turn to blood.

Rabbi Elijah, the Gaon of Vilna, was the greatest rabbinic authority of the eighteenth century, and widely respected for his scholarship. Setting out upon a journey to the Holy Land, he wrote a letter to his wife and mother from Koenigsberg. (When he reached Germany, Rabbi Elijah had a change of mind about his trip and returned home.) However, this letter has become famous for it reflects the attitude of this great man toward his wife, mother, and children. The following translation from the Hebrew original by Jossef Harlow is abridged.

I beg you to be neither grieved nor worried over my journey, as you have indeed promised me. There are men who travel many years to make their fortune, leaving their wives, to become homeless wanderers lacking everything. But I, thank God, am travelling to the Holy Land, which everybody hopes to see, the desired object of all Israel and of God, blessed be He. All creatures, above and below, long to see this land. I journey in peace, thank God, though as you realize I have left my children for whom my heart moans, and all my precious books, to become a stranger in another land.

It is a truism that this world is altogether vain and that all its delights are nothing. Woe to all who pursue profitless vanity. Do not be envious of wealth, for sometimes wealth is kept by its owner to his hurt. As man came from his mother's womb he shall go again, naked as he came, and he shall take nothing for his toil . . . just as he came so shall he go, and what gain has he that he toiled for the wind? . . . A man should be happy in all of the years which he lives, but he should remember that many days of darkness will follow; only emptiness will follow;—what can happiness do? For tomorrow he will cry louder than he laughs today. Do not envy apparent honor. Time is treacherous and, like scales, it can raise the light and lower the heavy. Man in this world might be spoken of as someone who is drinking a bowl of salt water. As he drinks his fill, he becomes thirstier. No man dies having possessed even one-half of his desires. "What does man gain by all the toil at which he toils under the sun?" Remember all those who have preceded us, and that all their desires and happiness have perished, and that they are severely judged for them. Man's end is dust and worms. The grave makes all of man's pleasures bitter; death and man are bound together. In this world, all man's days are anger and pain. Even at night they do not let him sleep. Yet he does not wish for death.

Man will be judged for every word that he utters; not even a chance phrase will go unaccounted for. Therefore I urge you to make solitude your habit, for sin through the tongue outweighs all other sins combined. Our sages, of blessed memory, stated that all of the commandments which a man might observe can not atone for the harm which he could cause with his mouth. . . .

On Sabbaths and festivals speak only of matters which are absolutely essential, and even in these instances be very brief, for the sanctity of the Sabbath is very great. The authorities were so concerned with this that only with great reluctance did they permit even an exchange of greetings on the Sabbath. Honor then the Sabbath to the utmost, as it was honored when I was with you.

I would also implore you that you train your daughters to avoid curses, oaths, lies, and contention. Let all of their conversations be conducted in peace, love, esteem, and gentleness. I have several books on morals, printed with German translations: let them read these constantly. Especially on the Sabbath, the holy of holies, should they be exclusively occupied with these books. Be strict in their moral training. This also applies to the avoidance of slander and gossip, and to the regular recital of grace before and after meals, and the reading of the *Shema*—everything thould be done in sincere devotion. The most fundamental rule is that they must not leave the house to walk about in the streets, God forbid, but rather that they obey and honor you and my mother and all of their elders.

Furthermore, raise your sons—may they have long life—in the right path and with gentleness. Maintain a teacher at home and pay him a decent salary. I have left some books for their use. Also, pay careful attention to their health and diet, so that they never lack anything. They should study the Pentateuch first, learning almost all of it by heart. Do not be too harsh with them, for instruction is effective only when it is conveyed in a gentle manner. Distribute presents of coins and the like to them. Give your constant attention to the rearing of the children, for everything else is vanity. . . .

Men are like herbage of the field: some bloom and others fade. Each person is born under a star and lives under the providence of the Most High God, blessed be He. When he dies, he descends to Sheol and leaves his possessions for enemies and strangers, who rejoice at his death. Woe to those who think that they will leave something for their children. The only profit one can see from sons and daughters is in their learning and in their good deeds. Their sustenance is provided by God.

Our sages stated that a good wife should do her husband's will. This should be especially so concerning the matters of which I write since they are derived from the words of the living God. I am certain that you would act as I have written in any case. Nevertheless I want to urge you doubly not to deviate from anything which I have requested. Read this letter every week, especially before the Sabbath meal or during the meal, so that the children will not engage in idle talk, God forbid, or in slander and the like at the table.

While training your sons and daughters in moral instruction, please let your words be tender, that you may win over their hearts. This is especially essential should we ever be privileged to settle in the Land of Israel, for there one must walk in the path of the Lord. Therefore, accustom them to the virtues I mention, for good speech and manners are qualities which demand training, until they become a matter of habit.

All beginnings are difficult. . . . The wicked man knows himself that his path is evil and bitter, but it is difficult for him to leave it. . . . A man needs to be chastened until the day of his death; and not by means of fasting or afflictions, but only by bridling his mouth. . . . Scripture states, "What man is there who desires life, and covets many days, that he may enjoy good? Keep your tongue from evil and your lips from speaking deceit." This will atone for every sin, and will save you from Sheol of the underworld, as it is written, "He who keeps his mouth and his tongue keeps himself out of trouble." Life and death are in the power of the tongue. Woe to him who destroys himself through one careless word. . . .

There is a German translation of the Book of Proverbs among my books. For the Lord's sake, let the children read in it every day; there is no better book for moral instruction. They should also read Ecclesiastes constantly and in your presence, for it puts the vanities of this world into proper perspective. In reading these and other books, the purpose should be more than merely reading, for no one is motivated to moral action by such a purpose. Many men read moral works which have no effect on them for this very reason.

Study in *Ethics of the Fathers* and especially in *The Fathers According to Rabbi Nathan* and in the tractate of *Derekh Eretz* takes precedence over the Torah. Treat your aged mother-in-law with great respect, and treat everyone with good manners, gentleness, and respect.

My beloved mother: I realize that you need no instruction from me, for I know of your modesty. Nevertheless, permit them to read this letter to you, for it contains advice derived from words of the living God. I earnestly implore you not to grieve for my sake, as you have promised. If by God's grace I should be privileged to reach Jerusalem, the Holy City, which is near the Gate of Heaven, I will pray for you, as I have promised. If the Merciful One wills it, all of us will soon be in the city together.

I ask my wife to honor my mother according to the precepts written in the Torah, especially regarding widows. It is really a criminal offense to trouble her, even in the smallest matter. I also entreat my mother to live in harmony with my wife, and each of you bring happiness to the other, for this is an important duty incumbent upon everyone. At Judgment, each person will be asked, "Have you been friendly in your relations with your fellow man?" The aim of the Torah, in large part, is to bring happiness to man. If either of you should offend the other, be forgiving, and live—for the Lord's sake—at peace. I request my mother that she advise my sons and my daughters in tender terms, that they may accept her teaching, and that she watch over them.

I ask my sons and my daughters to honor my mother, and I would have it that there be neither arguments nor anger between them, that peace may prevail. And may the Source of Peace grant you, my sons and my daughters, my sons-in-law and my brothers, and all Israel, life and peace.

These the words of one who loves you,

ELIJAH, SON OF SOLOMON ZALMAN

World War II saw the catastrophic extermination of European Jewry at the hands of Nazi Germany. Most of the hapless six million victims accepted martyrdom as inescapable. But there were exceptions—those who tried to fight back. Though they might not be able to save their lives, these brave persons felt that by their resistance, passive or active, they could serve as witnesses to the courage of their persecuted people.

Women played an important role in the underground resistance movement of the Jewish nationalist and socialist groups in Europe during World War II. The excerpt that follows, from Emmanuel Ringelblum's monumental contemporary record Notes from the Warsaw Ghetto *(published by McGraw-Hill), describes the girls who served as couriers on dangerous assignments for the Jewish underground.*

Fragment — Monument to Warsaw Ghetto Uprising by Nathan Rappaport (1947)

The heroic girls, Chajke and Frumke—they are a theme that calls for the pen of a great writer. Boldly they travel back and forth through the cities and towns of Poland. They carry "Aryan" papers identifying them as Poles or Ukrainians. One of them even wears a cross, which she never parts with except when in the Ghetto. They are in mortal danger every day. They rely entirely on their "Aryan" faces and on the peasant kerchiefs that cover their heads. Without a murmur, without a second's hesitation, they accept and carry out the most dangerous missions. Is someone needed to travel to Vilna, Bialystok, Lemberg, Kowel, Lublin, Czestochowa, or Radom to smuggle in contraband such as illegal publications, goods, money? The girls volunteer as though it were the most natural thing in the world. Are there comrades who have to be rescued from Vilna, Lublin, or some other city?—They undertake the mission.

Nothing stands in their way, nothing deters them. Is it necessary to become friendly with engineers of German trains, so as to be able to travel beyond the frontiers of the Government General of Poland, where people can move about with special papers? They are the ones to do it, simply, without fuss, as though it was their profession. They have traveled from city to city, to places no delegate or Jewish institution had ever reached, such as Wolhynia, Lithuania. They were the first to bring back the tidings about the tragedy of Vilna.* They were the first to offer words of encouragement and moral support to the surviving remnant of that city. How many times have they looked death in the eyes? How many times have they been arrested and searched? Fortune has smiled on them. They are, in the classic idiom, "emissaries of the community to whom no harm can come." With what simplicity and modesty have they reported what they accomplished on their journeys, on the trains bearing Polish Christians who have been pressed to work in Germany! The story of the Jewish woman will be a glorious page in the history of Jewry during the present war. And the Chajkes and Frumkes will be the leading figures in this story. For these girls are indefatigable. Just back from Czestochowa, where they imported contraband, in a few hours they'll be on the move again. And they're off without a moment's hesitation, without a minute of rest.

135

From the days of the pioneers to the War of Independence and the subsequent building of the nation, its culture and industry, the women of Israel have labored and achieved side by side with their menfolk. Capable in peace, valiant in war, their devotion unmatched among modern womankind, they have written a glorious chapter in the history of Israel and of all humanity.

Since June 1956 Golda (Meyerson) Meir has served as foreign minister of Israel. She is the only woman to hold this post in any of the democratic countries.

She was born in Kiev, Russia. When she was eight the family migrated to Milwaukee, Wisconsin, where Golda grew up to become a school teacher. A Zionist from her early youth, she married Morris Meyerson on the condition that they go to Palestine. Arriving there in 1921, they joined the kibbutz Merhavia, where Golda was trained as a specialist in poultry raising.

Her political career was long and varied. She held important positions in the Women's Labor Council, in Histadrut, the General Federation of Labor, and as head of the Jewish Agency Political Department.

At the end of 1948, Golda Meyerson became Israel's first ambassador to Russia. She was recalled to Israel in 1949 to become Minister of Labor in Prime Minister Ben Gurion's first cabinet. In June 1956, upon the resignation of Moshe Sharett, Golda Meir (in keeping with Israel practice, she Hebraized her name) assumed the office of Minister for Foreign Affairs.   In 1969 she became Prime Minister of Israel.

GOLDA MEIR
1898 -

It was a time of Nazi terror, when Jews were being murdered by scores of thousands in every country where the Swastika of Hitler reigned. To escape to Palestine was the only hope.

Hannah Szenes was a young Hungarian woman who *had* escaped, just before the second world war began in 1939. She lived and worked in Palestine. But her mother was still in Hungary, and so were thousands of other Jews. The Jewish Agency believed that resistance could be organized, and rescue centers established, to smuggle them out to Palestine.

To organize a rescue operation, it was necessary that Palestine Jews be parachuted into the Balkans. It would be dangerous. They must be Jews of great courage and determination. The British Command agreed to drop them if they would also do intelligence work for the Allies.

Hannah Szenes was one of thirty-two volunteers dropped over the Balkans in March, 1944. She and two others were picked up by Hungarian resistance fighters. But when these anti-Nazis learned that the parachuted volunteers were Jews, they handed over Hannah and the others to Hitler's Gestapo. The two men managed to escape, but Hannah was executed as a spy in November, 1944.

She lives in Jewish history as a heroine. A book by the noted writer, Marie Syrkin, called *Blessed Is the Match*, tells her story.

HANNAH SZENES
1921-1944

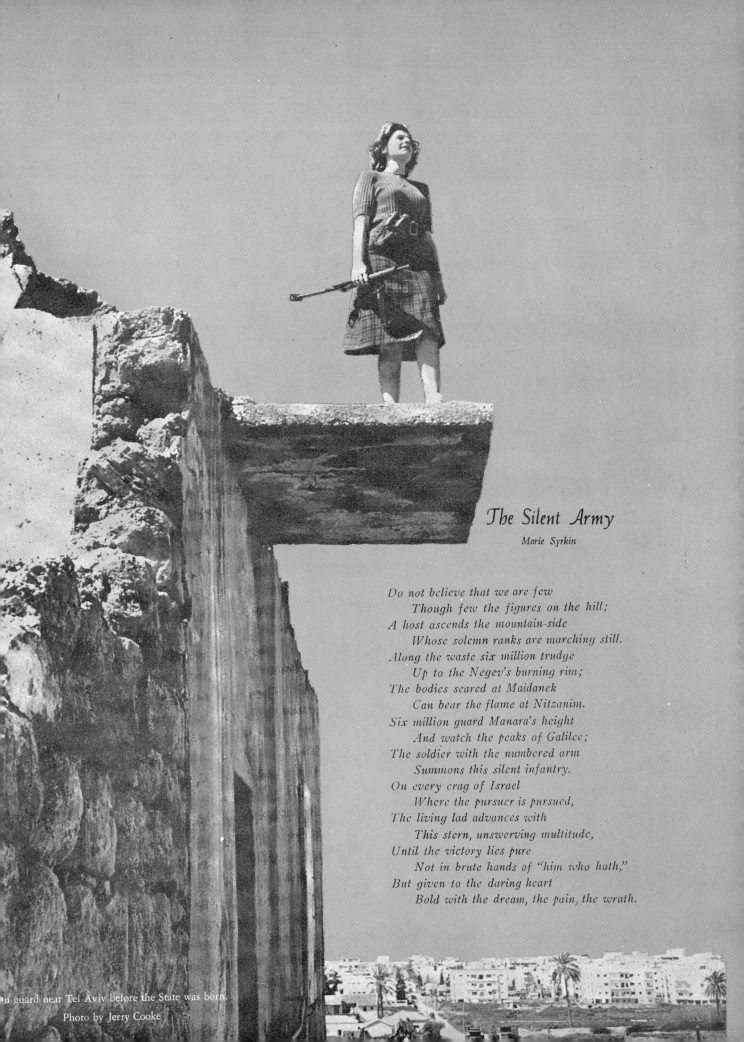

The Silent Army

Marie Syrkin

Do not believe that we are few
  Though few the figures on the hill;
A host ascends the mountain-side
  Whose solemn ranks are marching still.
Along the waste six million trudge
  Up to the Negev's burning rim;
The bodies seared at Maidanek
  Can bear the flame at Nitzanim.
Six million guard Manara's height
  And watch the peaks of Galilee;
The soldier with the numbered arm
  Summons this silent infantry.
On every crag of Israel
  Where the pursuer is pursued,
The living lad advances with
  This stern, unswerving multitude,
Until the victory lies pure
  Not in brute hands of "him who hath,"
But given to the daring heart
  Bold with the dream, the pain, the wrath.

n guard near Tel Aviv before the State was born.

Photo by Jerry Cooke

In no other country do women play so important a role among their people as in Israel. Every sphere of human activity — science, agriculture, the arts, literature, government, even the military — is represented in the roster of their activities.

Young woman picking cotton.

Courtesy Israel Office of Information

A fighter in time of war; a builder in time of peace.

Courtesy Jesse Zel Lurie

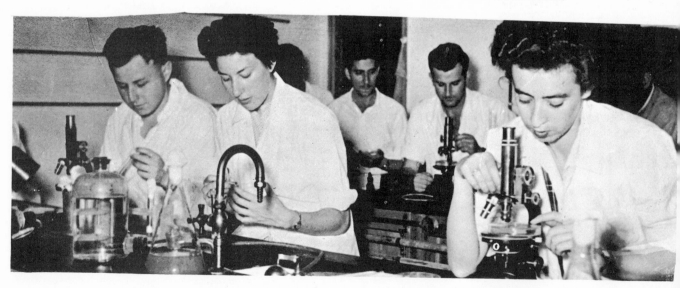

In cultural life and in the expansion of industry, the Israeli woman takes a prominent part.

Courtesy American Technion Society

THE TWELVE TRIBES, EMANATING FROM THE INITIALS OF THE FATHERS, Mosaic by A. Raymond Katz, made for Beth Yehuda Synagogue, Lock Haven, Pennsylvania.

HIGHLIGHTS OF THE HISTORY OF THE JEWS

by Meyer Waxman

The Jews Become a Nation

The history of the Jewish people differs in many respects from those of other nations. Jewish history extends far into the past, whereas most nations are of relatively recent origin. It also encompasses nearly the entire earth, for Jewish communities have existed in almost every country of the world at one time or another. Because of its large extent in time and space, the Jewish story is marked by a multitude of important events which reflect the history of all humanity.

The history of the Jews as a nation began in the Sinai Desert, when the Israelites, who had just been liberated from the bondage of Egypt, received the Torah on Mt. Sinai. The Torah is, in effect, the Jewish constitution. It provides both the laws to be observed and the ideals to be attained. By means of these laws and ideals, the mass of former slaves were unified and made distinct from the other nations of that time. Indeed, the laws of the Torah basically differed from their laws. It prohibited worship of idols, which all other peoples then practiced, and substituted the belief in one unseeable God, Creator of the world. The value of human life, then everywhere disregarded, was proclaimed sacred by the Torah, because man was created in the image of God. Respect and consideration were commanded for strangers and foreigners. The Sabbath was instituted, which taught that every seventh day was holy and was to be devoted to rest and to spiritual pursuits. The Torah also contains detailed regulations regarding the government of the people and the duties of the individual toward God, toward the government, and toward mankind. The Torah thus became the Law and the strength of the Jews. Armed with it, they ascended the stage of history, where they played an outstanding and unique role.

The Judges

The Land of Canaan had long been divinely promised to the Jewish people. After they had wandered in the Sinai Desert for forty years, the Jews entered Canaan under the leadership of Joshua, Moses' disciple. But occupation of the country was not an easy matter. Nearly two hundred years elapsed before it became theirs. During this time the Jews engaged in many struggles. Canaan had strong fortified cities that had to be conquered. Before these were taken, the Jewish tribes were separated from one another. This gave rise to the institution of "Judges." Each tribe lived under the leadership of a Judge whom they obeyed, and who led them in war against their enemies. There were many great leaders among them, but not one succeeded in unifying all the tribes into a single government.

During this time the Jews also found it difficult to resist the influence of their Canaanite neighbors. Though they possessed a great spiritual treasure in the Torah, their material civilization was poor, because they had but recently emerged from a state of slavery. The Canaanites, on the other hand, were a wealthy people living in well-built cities and enjoying the comforts of civilization. Many Jews fell under the spell of this civilization and forgot the teachings of the Torah. When admonished by their leaders, they would return temporarily to the ways of God as taught in the Torah, but they frequently slipped back.

The Prophetess Deborah, and her military leader Barak, largely completed the conquest of the country. Unification of the nation was nearly achieved. A central sanctuary was established in Shiloh. But there still existed no central government. The Judges still ruled over single tribes, or groups of tribes.

The Rise of the Kingdom

Samuel, last of the Judges and priest-prophet, yielded to the demands of the people that a king be appointed to rule them. He did so reluctantly, pointing out the disadvantages of an all-powerful monarch. But when the people insisted, he anointed Saul as the first king over Israel. Saul ruled for twenty years. He was successful in many of his wars against the Philistines, but his reign ended tragically. This was due to a number of causes. Saul disobeyed the commands of God as voiced by Samuel. He also became jealous of the young hero David, who had distinguished himself when he slew the Philistine champion Goliath. Irked by David's rising popularity, Saul became mentally ill. Because of the king's growing jealousy, David was forced to flee and gather a following of his own. These events diminished Saul's power, and together with his son Jonathan he was killed in a battle against the Philistines.

After a brief interregnum, David became king. Though marked by a number of rebellions, his reign was glorious. He decisively defeated the Philistines; he took the last unconquered fortress of the Jebusites and established there the city of

Jerusalem, which became the eternal capital of Israel. He extended his conquests far and wide.

The personality of David became a model for all future Jewish rulers. Though subject to sudden passions, David's repentance was so profound and sincere that a prophet assured eternity to David's dynasty. Deeply pious, David expressed his feelings in the world's most beautiful hymns, which are included in the Book of Psalms. David wanted to use the great wealth he acquired for construction of a Temple, but he was told that he could not build it, because he had shed too much blood. Instead the Temple would be built by his son, Solomon, a king of peace.

During Solomon's reign the glory of the kingdom reached its height. He preserved the empire his father had built, by means of efficient administration and alliances with neighboring states. These policies brought him peace. Solomon made Israel a prosperous commercial center. With the help of Hiram, king of Tyre, he sent fleets of ships to distant lands to transport gold and precious stones. Much of these riches was used for building the Temple.

Solomon is remembered for his wisdom. He was also a great poet. Three books in the Bible, The Song of Songs, Ecclesiastes, and Proverbs, are said to have been written by him. But Solomon's rule was also marred by injudicious acts which led to tragedy. His marriages to foreign princesses brought on a partial revival of idolatry, and the heavy taxes he levied to maintain the splendor of his court aroused much dissatisfaction, especially in the northern part of the kingdom.

The Kingdom Divided in Two

When Solomon died, the northern ten tribes broke away and set up a separate kingdom called Israel. The tribes of Judah and Benjamin remained loyal to Solomon's son, who ruled over the kingdom of Judah. This political division was not the only rift among the people. The division of Solomon's kingdom was also accompanied by a spiritual breach. In order to dissuade the people of Israel from visiting the Temple in Jerusalem, the king of Israel, Jeroboam, set up two sanctuaries in his own realm. These were originally intended for the worship of God, but gradually this was contaminated by the introduction of idols, leading to a revival of idolatry throughout Israel. From this time on, life in Israel presented a continuous struggle between the prophets representing true religion, and the princes and kings who constantly lapsed into idolatry.

Nor was the political life of Israel a happy one. The rebellion against Solomon's son set an example for ambitious men later, and revolts were a frequent occurrence, each bringing to the throne a new dynasty. Still, during the two hundred years of the kingdom of Israel, there were also considerable periods of peace and prosperity.

Far to the northeast of Israel and Judah the Assyrian Empire began to expand. It subjected all small nations in its way. For a time Israel submitted, but when, relying on aid from Egypt, King Hosea ben Ela rebelled, the Assyrians besieged Samaria, capital of Israel, and captured it three years later. True to the policy of the Assyrian conquerors, Sargon exiled a part of the people to a distant land, and in their place settled folk from other lands. These people adopted some of the precepts of Judaism. They became known as "Samaritans." A handful remain to this day in the city of Schechem, now known as Nablus.

The Kingdom of Judah

The kingdom of Judah existed much longer. There was one Davidic dynasty and the majority of the kings followed true Judaism. Assyria also came into Judah and subjected it for a time. King Hezekiah rebelled, relying on Egypt's promises. The Assyrian king, Sennacherib, besieged Jerusalem, but the city was miraculously saved when the Assyrian army, stricken by plague, was forced to retire. That ended Assyria's rule. The reigns of Hezekiah and Jehoash were periods of great religious revival. After Assyria, Babylonia came into Judah, and for a short time, King Jehoiakim submitted to these masters. But soon he too rebelled and the Babylonians besieged Jerusalem and exiled his son, Jehoiachin, and part of the people. Zedekiah then became king; when he revolted, the siege was renewed. Jerusalem fell — 586 B.C.E. The Temple was burned and the people were exiled.

The Prophets

The period of the kings was distinguished by the activity of the prophets. Prophecy became a factor in Jewish life at the time of Samuel, but its effects grew more pronounced after Elijah. Inspired by the divine spirit, all the prophets fought against idolatry and insisted on ethical conduct. They feared no one and chastised the rich and the powerful for their wrongdoing. So great was their moral authority that even powerful kings like Ahab trembled before their wrath. Amos emphasized the universality of God. Isaiah foretold the spread of knowledge of God throughout the world, and the reign of peace on earth when "nation shall not lift up sword against nation." Jeremiah taught the eternity of the Jewish people. All the prophets told of a bright future, "in the end of days," the days of the Messiah. The words of the prophets are a great spiritual and moral heritage not only for the Jewish people, but for all humanity.

The Second Commonwealth

The exile of the Jews in Babylonia lasted only forty-seven years — a short time, when compared with the later Jewish dispersion. But its effects on Jewish history were great. Surprisingly, it was in their Babylonian exile that the Jews once and for all renounced all pagan beliefs and practices, and became unwavering believers in pure monotheism.

SILVER SHEKEL OF THE FIRST REVOLT (66-70 C.E.)
Obverse: Chalice with knob on stem. Inscription: Shekel of Israel, Year 3.
Reverse: Stem with bunch of three pomegranates. Inscription: "Jerusalem the Holy"

As a people they never relapsed again. The Babylonian exile also marked the beginning of the Jewish Diaspora. When Cyrus of Persia, who had conquered Babylonia, permitted the exiles to return, only a small number traveled to Jerusalem with their leader Zerubabel — 42,300 all told. Another thousand returned later with Ezra the scribe. The majority remained in Babylonia and in neighboring countries, without losing their loyalty to Judaism. Those who returned succeeded in rebuilding the Temple in the year 516 B.C.E.

We do not know much about the hundred years that elapsed from the death of Ezra and Nehemiah to the conquest of the country by Alexander the Great. We do know that the Jews enjoyed autonomy in Eretz Israel under Persian suzerainty. They were headed by a governing body called "The Great Assembly," which in turn was headed by the high priest. Much intellectual activity was carried on by a group known as *Soferim* (Scribes), who interpreted the Torah and made it fit the conditions of life at that time. Many laws which had been passed on orally and were known to only a few, were now revealed to all the people. During the era of the Scribes and the Great Assembly, the daily prayers and the public reading of the Law on Sabbaths and other days were instituted.

Independence

The Jews first met the Greeks when Alexander the Great conquered the East. At first Palestine (or Judea) was governed by the Greek rulers of Egypt. Later the Greek kings of Syria took the country from Egypt. Greek culture was highly develloped and the aristocratic families of Jewish society fell under its spell. A process of assimilation set in. When Antiochus Epiphanes ascended the throne of Syria, he undertook to force the Greek way of life upon all Jews. The Temple was desecrated with a statue of Zeus, and Jews were forbidden to practice the most important rites of their religion. This led to a rebellion under the leadership of Mattathias the Hasmonean, a priest of the city of Modin, and his five sons. Judah, most valiant of Mattathias' sons, succeeded in defeating the Greeks and rededicating the Temple in 165 B.C.E. This occasion gave rise to the festival of Chanukah.

The struggle for independence went on for a considerable time. Judah was killed in one of the battles, but his brother Jonathan succeeded in winning autonomy. Simon, another of Mattathias' sons, won full independence and established the Maccabean — or Hasmonean — dynasty which ruled the country for 103 years.

Subjection

This was a time of strength and expansion for the Jewish State, but there was also much internal strife. Various parties appeared on the scene. There were the Sadducees, who consisted largely of aristocrats. The Pharisees, a people's party, broadly interpreted the Torah laws to apply to all details of life. The conflicts between these parties often led to strife and even to civil war. This provided the huge and expanding Roman empire an opportunity to intervene.

The Jewish princelings who contended for the throne brought their dispute before

143

Pompey, a Roman general. Pompey utilized his position as arbitrator to impose Roman rule. In 63 B.C.E. he entered Jerusalem. For a time, descendants of the Hasmoneans continued to rule under Roman tutelage. Then the Romans made Herod king of Judea. Herod's sympathies were largely with the Romans. His reign was materially prosperous, but he ruled with an iron hand, and committed many crimes, including the murder of his wife Miriam, a descendant of the Hasmoneans, and their two sons. After Herod's death, Judea became a Roman province.

Roman rule in Judea was oppressive, and in 66 C.E. a great rebellion broke out. Not all the Jews were of the same mind concerning the revolt. Some wished to fight for outright independence; others were in favor of making peace with Rome, realizing that it was impossible to defeat the mighty Roman empire.

In 67 the Roman general, Vespasian, undertook to subdue the rebel Jews. His son, Titus, besieged Jerusalem in the spring of 70 C.E. The beleaguered Jews, short of food and water, fought valiantly against the numerous and well-armed Roman legions. They held out for six months. Toward the end of the siege both food and water were completely gone. Still they fought, retreating to a successive series of fortresses when driven from more advanced posts. The Romans had the most modern instruments of siege of that day. The Jews had their faith and their determination. On the ninth day of Av, the part of the city still in Jewish hands fell to the Romans. The Temple was burned and the city was destroyed.

Spiritual and Cultural Life

Throughout this period, there was great spiritual activity. Study of the Torah and Oral Law increasingly became the all-embracing interest of large masses. The government itself was conducted with the help of the Sanhedrin, a parliament of scholars and important laymen. The scholars interpreted the religious, civil, and criminal laws of Judaism. The laymen dealt with political and administrative matters. Most of the members were of the Pharisaic party. The scholarly section was headed by a president and dean. At the time of Herod, there lived the great Hillel, a man of remarkable character. His statement: "That which is hateful unto thyself, do not do unto others," became a cardinal principle of Jewish ethics.

The New Concept of Judaism

The Romans struck a special medal after the conquest of Jerusalem, which read "Judaea Capta" — Judea is captured. True, Judea had been conquered, the State was gone, but the nation was not destroyed. Many Jews remained in Eretz Israel; a large number lived in other lands, in Babylonia, Egypt, and Rome itself. The Torah and Judaism became the fatherland of the Jews, and hope for redemption and faith in the coming of Messiah became strong factors in Jewish survival.

To keep the Jewish people united wherever they were, a spiritual center was necessary, and that center was provided by the great scholar Johanan ben Zakkai, a disciple of Hillel, who left Jerusalem some time before its destruction and established an Academy at Jabneh. There gathered many scholars, who reconstituted the

Sanhedrin, which exercised authority in all religious, civil, and social matters affecting Jews over the world. It standardized the important prayers and made prayer the main form of worship. When Johanan died, the presidency of the Sanhedrin passed to descendants of Hillel.

Soon a new storm broke. The longing of the people for independence could not easily be put down. A rebellion led by Simeon bar Kochba attracted a large number of followers, among them the greatest spiritual leader and scholar of the age, Rabbi Akiba. Within a year, Roman rule was swept out of the country, Jerusalem was recaptured, and a Jewish government established. Rome sent its best general and many legions, and after a bitter struggle of two years the last stronghold, Bethar, fell, and Simeon was killed. The number of Jews slain ran into hundreds of thousands, the cities destroyed into hundreds. Hadrian took cruel revenge. He aimed to wipe out Judaism, and severe punishment was meted out upon all observers, especially those who taught the Torah. Rabbi Akiba challenged the Roman decree and died a martyr while teaching. He thus inspired later generations of Jews to undergo martyrdom for their religion.

When Antoninus Pius revoked Hadrian's decrees in 138 C.E., life became normal again to some extent. The Academy and the Sanhedrin moved to Galilee and continued their activity. But the effects of the rebellion were evident; the population had decreased, poverty prevailed, and emigration to other lands assumed large proportions. It was then that Judah the Prince, head of the Academy, decided to compile a work that would stabilize Judaism all over the world. In collaboration with other scholars, he edited the Mishnah, in six parts. Hitherto, the extensive Jewish law had been orally taught in various schools, and this gave rise to many differences. Now a written text was made available to all scholars.

Eretz Israel and Babylonia

During the next three hundred years there were two centers of world Jewry. There arose the center in Babylonia, where the Jewish population was large, and economic and political conditions were favorable. Learning had been cultivated there before, but it rose to still greater heights when Aba Arika, a student of Judah the Prince, returned with the Mishnah and opened an Academy at Sura. His colleague, Samuel, taught at Nehardea, and Rab Yehudah, a disciple of both, founded the Academy at Pumpbedita (247 C.E.). The heads of the Academies, as well as other outstanding scholars, were called *amoraim,* commentators, for they interpreted the Mishnah.

Similar activity went on in Palestine. Here, too, *amoraim* expounded the Mishnah and elucidated regulations for the Jewish way of life. For a time, these exerted influence upon Jewish settlements in Egypt, Arabia, and the early communities in southern Europe. But soon the political situation worsened. The Roman empire became officially Christian and began to persecute the Jews. For a short time, though, a ray of light broke forth. The Roman emperor, Julian, who is called the apostate, for he preferred paganism to Christianity, favored the Jews and wanted to rebuild the Temple. His plan was not carried out, and he died shortly thereafter in battle (362). The situation under succeeding emperors grew worse, and learning diminished. In the reign of Theodosius II, the Academies were closed.

As the influence of Palestine declined, the Babylonian center gained in importance, especially after the Talmud was compiled. As generations of teachers continued to expound the law, it became necessary to collect and write down all the accepted interpretations and discussions. This work — the Talmud — was a complished in 352-427 C.E. by a group of scholars under the guidance of Rab Ashi.

The Talmud includes the Mishnah plus all the comments and explanations of generations of scholars. The comments are called Gemara. It contains not only laws for regulating Jewish social life, but also ethical teachings, historical information, and stories about the deeds of great men of all generations. The Talmud is divided into sixty-three tractates, each dealing with a separate subject. It was finished in the year 500 C.E. and became Jewry's primary literature supplementing the Bible.

The Period of the Geonim

The post-talmudic period, 500-1038 C.E., is marked by important events in Jewish history. For several centuries, Babylonia remained a center of influence in world Jewry. The heads of the two Babylonian academies, called *geonim,* after the Talmud was compiled, continued to guide many communities in Asia and in Europe. But, many changes entered into the life of Babylonian Jewry through the emergence of a new religion and a new political power. This religion is known as Mohammedanism, or Islam. After the death of its founder, Mohammed (632 C.E.), the new faith was spread by force of arms over much of Asia, part of Africa, and Spain in Europe. The Jews of Palestine, Egypt, Babylonia, and all other parts of the Persian empire came under Moslem rule. The language of the conquerors was Arabic, and they developed an extensive culture in Babylonia and many other countries.

This new turn of events radically changed Jewish life. Arabic became the spoken language of the Jews, though they did not forget Hebrew and continued to cherish it. They also began to develop a rich literature of Bible commentaries, Hebrew grammar, and philosophy. In this field the work of Saadia Gaon (892-942 C.E.) is most distinguished. A great part of the literature was composed in Arabic, or Judaeo-Arabic, but many works were also written in Hebrew.

About the middle of the eighth century, a man named Anan founded a sect which claimed literal obedience to the Bible and rejected the Talmud — or the Oral Law. His followers called themselves Karaites, from the Hebrew word *mikra* — the Scriptures. The sect spread through other countries, but won over only a fraction of the Jews. A small number still exist today.

Two medieval Jewish kingdoms were founded by gentile converts in both the Arabic and Christian worlds. One, in Arabia of the pre-Islamic period, lasted about thirty years. Its last king, Joseph Dhu Nuwas, died 525 C.E. in a war with the Chris-

146

tians of Ethiopia. The other was the kingdom of the Khazars, a Mongolian people who lived in the steppes of the Volga. They were converted to Judaism about 740 C.E. and their kingdom lasted for some centuries, until it was overrun by the Russians.

Toward the end of this period, Jewish settlements in Spain, Italy, France, and Germany began to take ascendancy in Jewish life. The Babylonian center gradually lost its prestige, and its population began to diminish. The Academies were closed (1038 C.E.) and the office of the Gaon ceased to exist.

The Middle Ages

For Jews, the Middle Ages occupy the the span of time from 1000 C.E. to 1750 C.E. This period marked the rise of Jewish centers in Europe, first in southern and western Europe, and later in eastern Europe. With few exceptions, this was a time of great physical suffering, but also of vast intellectual activity, resulting in an extensive literature.

Throughout Europe, the Jews had few rights, and were barely tolerated by kings, princes, and feudal lords. Expulsions from cities and countries are too numerous to be listed here; the same holds true for assaults and massacres. But one must mention the First Crusade and the religious fanaticism and Jew-hatred it created. In 1096, the Jews in northern France and Germany were attacked and massacred by the Crusaders. The number of the slain is estimated as 12,000 — at least one third of the Jews in Germany. This was followed by the Second (1146), Third (1187), and Fourth (1202 — 4) Crusades, during which Jews were everywhere massacred. In 1290, the Jews were expelled from England, and in 1394 from France. When the Black Death spread through Europe (1348-50) and killed twenty-five million people, Jews, falsely accused of poisoning the wells, were again brutally massacred. In 1391, the people of Spain, excited by fanatics, attacked the Jews, half of whom were either killed or forcibly converted. This marks the beginning of the *Marrano-Jews* who outwardly professed Christianity while secretly observing Judaism. The year 1492 saw the expulsion of all the Jews from Spain (about 200,000). Many died from starvation or disease and a number settled in North Africa, Turkey, Palestine, and several European countries. A century later, in 1593, Marrano Jews also settled in Holland.

Cossack Massacres

The large settlement of Jews in Poland suffered disaster in the years 1648-50, when the Cossacks, under Chmielnicki, rebelled against the Poles, and destroyed many Jewish communities on the assumption that Jews were too friendly to the Poles. It is estimated that a quarter of a million Jews perished. The miracle of Jewish survival, under such circumstances, is to be explained by steadfast devotion to religion and ideals, and by strong belief in the coming redemption and the return to the Holy Land, as promised by the prophets.

Cultural Flowering

In those countries where Jews were better treated, they took part in the general life and developed their own culture to a high degree. The years from 1000 to 1200 in Spain, we call the Golden Age. Solomon ibn Gabirol (1021-1058), Bachya ibn Pakuda (fl. 1050), and Judah ha-Levi (1085-1142) wrote philosophical books in Arabic, and Judah Halevi's magnificent poems won him the title of sweet singer of Zion. Abraham ibn Ezra (1093-1167) wrote excellent commentaries on the Bible, books on astronomy, and Hebrew poems. Maimonides (Moses ben Maimon, born in Spain 1135, died in Egypt 1204), greatest of medieval Jews, composed outstanding books on medicine; a great philosophic work "Guide For the Perplexed" in Judaeo-Arabic; and a comprehensive code of Jewish law (Mishneh Torah) in Hebrew.

Among Jews of France and Germany, the intellectual activity was carried on in Hebrew, consisting in study of the Bible, the Talmud, and rabbinic law. Translations from Judaeo-Arabic into Hebrew had been made of the great Jewish works. There was Rabbi Gershom, "Light of the Exile" (960-1040), among whose many ordinances were those promulgating monogamy and regulating divorce. Here, too, lived Solomon ben Isaac (1040-1105), known as *Rashi,* whose commentaries on the Bible and the Talmud clarified the texts and made them readily available to students to this very day. Joseph Karo of Spain (1488-1575), who settled in Palestine after the expulsion, compiled a complete code of Jewish law called *Shulhan Arukh,* which is still the standard for traditional Judaism.

False Messiahs

Whenever great suffering occurred, messianic movements arose. The period from 1492 to the end of the 18th century produced a number of such movements. The most important was that of Sabbetai Zevi (1620-1676) which originated in Smyrna (Turkey) and attracted followers among Jews everywhere. It ended disastrously, when the leader, seized by the Turks, accepted Islam. He died a prisoner in an Albanian fortress. In 1759, another movement arose in southern Poland, headed by Jacob Frank. It, too, attracted many followers and ended similarly by the conversion of Frank and his disciples to Catholicism.

Hassidism

In the eighteenth century a new and powerful movement arose among Jews in eastern Europe. This was *Hassidism.* The founder of the movement was Rabbi Israel Baal Shem Tov — "Master of the Good Name" (1700-1759). The basic principle of this movement was that piety and love of God were fully as important as scholarly disputation. As a result of this principle, *hassidim* ascribed as great worth to fervent prayer as to study of talmudic law. Hassidism spread rapidly because it appealed to the poor masses of Jews, many of whom lacked the time for scholarly pursuits.

The successors of Israel Baal Shem Tov gained wide followings, and hassidic congregations soon arose in hundreds of towns. These were like great brotherhoods. The members were devoted to one another.

The hassidic rabbis came to be known as *Zaddikim* (from the Hebrew word for "righteous"). Many of these were truly great men, and their ethical teachings have influenced Jewish life and literature to this day. But some of their followers tended to become too dependent on their rabbis, and to look upon them as miracle workers. Most of the Jews, called *mitnagdim* (opponents), feared that the new movement might undermine study and observance by too great stress on mere emotion. The mitnagdim were also displeased by the great reverence which the hassidim accorded their rabbis. They feared that unless this trend was checked, it might lead to worship of their rabbis as "saints," a principle that is alien to Judaism. The altercations between *hassidim* and *mitnagdim* resulted in much bitterness. Eventually these two major trends in Judaism became reconciled, and the *hassidim* with their appreciation of "the wonder of Jewish life" richly complemented the *mitnagdim* with their strict adherence to "the law of Jewish life." Similarly, the opponents encouraged the *hassidim* to greater interest in study.

The End of the Ghetto (1750-1880)

By the middle of the eighteenth century, the ideas of liberty, equality, and fraternity prevalent in Europe also began to penetrate the Jewish communities of western Europe, and aroused a desire to adjust to the new conditions. This movement was spurred by Moses Mendelssohn (1729-1786), a Jewish philosopher and distinguished writer in the German language. Under his influence Jews began to participate in German culture. This latter movement was called *Haskalah,* which means Enlightenment. It sought to arouse a greater interest in secular learning — literature, science, and art.

The revolution which swept France at the end of the eighteenth century aroused in the Jews a desire to obtain equal rights. For a short time during the reign of Napoleon, the Jews of Germany enjoyed such rights, and this taste of freedom prompted them to introduce changes in their own Jewish modes, to resemble those of their neighbors. This desire was the basis of the "Reform" movement, which denied that Jews were a nation, and declared that the Jews of Germany were simply Germans practicing the Mosaic religion.

Persecution in Russia

The struggle for equal rights for Jews met with considerable success in western Europe, but in the east the situation was different. Most Jews of Poland became subjects of the Russian Empire when Poland was largely annexed by Russia. The Russian rulers were hostile toward the Jews. The people were permitted to live only in a small section of Russia known as the Pale of Settlement. During the reign of Nicholas I (1825-1855) young Jewish boys were pressed into military service for twenty-five years. Except for a brief interlude during the reign of Alexander II, the Jews of Russia were constantly oppressed and persecuted.

Creative Cultural Life

But even though they had to suffer great hardships, the Jews of Russia led a creative religious life. Learning flourished and many *yeshivot* (talmudic academies) were established. The *Haskalah* movement gained ground and brought about a true renaissance of Hebrew literature. Many Hebrew newspapers and magazines were founded and prospered. Outstanding Hebrew novelists, like Abraham Mapu (1805-

1867) and Peretz Smolenskin (1842-1885), and gifted poets like Micah Joseph Lebensohn (1828-1852) and Judah Leib Gordon (1831-1892) appeared on the scene.

Emigration

Toward the end of the nineteenth century profound events occurred in Jewish life in Europe. Anti-Semitism became prevalent in western Europe, especially in Germany. In Russia hatred of the Jews assumed the form of physical violence, and many pogroms, in which Jews were murdered and robbed, took place in the early eighteen-eighties.

The pogroms and the new repressions that followed reawakened the Jews of Russia to an appreciation of their true situation. Many who had believed that modern civilization would bring them freedom and equal rights, now realized that their situation was hopeless, and that they would always remain scapegoats. This gave rise to two social movements. One was emigration — flight from Russia. This mass migration was directed largely to the United States, though smaller numbers also went to England and South Africa.

The second movement maintained that security and freedom for Jews to live as Jews could be assured only in the Jewish Homeland. This movement was largely influenced by Leo Pinsker (1821-1891), M.L. Lilienblum (1843-1910), and Rabbi Samuel Mohilever (1824-1898). Small groups called *Hoveve Zion* (Lovers of Zion) were organized, and a number of young men traveled to Palestine to establish agricultural settlements.

Zionism

In 1896, Dr. Theodor Herzl, a Jewish journalist from Vienna, came to Paris to report the trial of Captain Dreyfus. The Dreyfus case, which aroused the interest of the entire world, involved a Jewish officer in the French army falsely accused of treason and sentenced to a long term of imprisonment. (He was ultimately exonerated.) While Dreyfus was on trial, the case was used to fan anti-Jewish hatred. Dr. Herzl became convinced that the only solution to the Jewish problem was the establishment of a Jewish State where Jews could govern themselves. He wrote a book called *Judenstaat* (Jewish State) in which he presented his views. This created a tremendous stir. In 1897, Herzl convoked the first World Zionist Congress, in which Jews from all countries participated. The Congress founded the World Zionist Organization. Herzl conducted negotiations with the Sultan of Turkey (then ruler of Palestine) to obtain the rights to an autonomous settlement of Jews in Palestine. He also visited the rulers of many countries in an effort to win their support for Zionism. Herzl's negotiations were not successful, but many Jews recognized him as their spokesman.

After Herzl died in 1904, the movement continued its work. Many settlements were established in Palestine. Following the 1905 pogroms in Russia, emigration to Palestine gained much momentum. The Zionist movement also conducted extensive educational work. In Palestine, Eliezer ben Yehudah (1858-1922) undertook to make Hebrew the spoken language of the people. His efforts were successfully continued by others. Today Hebrew is the language of the Jews in Israel, and is studied wherever Jews live in freedom.

Two World Wars

In 1914 the First World War broke out. Jews suffered heavily, because so many of them lived in Poland and Russia, where many great battles were fought. When the war ended, Poland was again set up as an independent country, but the Jews of Russia were cut off from the rest of the world as a result of the Bolshevik Revolution. For a short period in 1918, that part of southern Russia known as the Ukraine was independent, and hundreds of thousands of Jews were massacred there.

When the world finally regained some semblance of normalcy after World War I, the Jewish people in eastern Europe found themselves in a sad state. Perhaps the only positive outcome of this war for the Jews, was the issuance of the Balfour Declaration (1917), wherein the British government undertook to make Palestine again the Jewish National Home. The other countries of the world followed suit. The Zionist movement expanded greatly and much work was done in Palestine. Great stretches of desert and swamp land were reclaimed. Cities and villages were established. Scholarship was fostered and a variety of institutions of higher learning were established.

Catastrophe in Europe

But the years of relative peace did not last long. The Jews of Poland, Romania, and Hungary were made to suffer increasing persecution, and a new enemy, more terrible than any before, appeared on the horizon.

In Germany an obscure former corporal named Hitler incited the people against the Jews and gained a great following. His popularity grew so rapidly that by 1933 he became Premier of Germany, and his party, the Nazis, ruled the country. He at once instituted the most terrible dictatorship in history. All the people were denied freedom, but his chief hatred was directed against the Jews of the world.

The Second World War broke out in 1939 when Germany invaded Poland. Within a short time Hitler's armies occupied nearly all of Europe. The greatest crime in history was then committed by the Germans. Millions of Jews were gassed by the Germans in specially constructed "extermination centers." Others were tortured to death. Children and infants were not spared.

By the time World War II ended, six million Jews of Europe — more than one-third of all the Jews in the world — had been slaughtered by the Germans under Hitler.

The one and one-half million Jews who survived in Europe found themselves in horrendous predicament. Most had lost their families. They did not wish to return to their native towns. Temporarily they stayed in what were called "Displaced Persons' Camps." They wanted to migrate to Palestine, but the Arabs opposed their admission and the British rulers of Palestine admitted only an insignificant number.

The Jews of Palestine came to their aid, and thousands of surviving European Jews were brought into the land contrary to the wishes of both British and Arabs. Most of the people in the world sympathized with the plight of the Jews. In November, 1947, the United Nations adopted a resolution approving the division of Palestine into two independent countries, one Jewish and the other Arab.

*　　*　　*

In April, 1948, the Jews of Palestine proclaimed their independence and opened the gates of their little country, which they named "Israel," to all Jews who wished to come there. The United States first, and many other nations, recognized the new republic. But at once all the Arab countries attacked Israel. It was an uneven struggle; the Jews were outnumbered forty to one. The United Nations failed to come to the aid of Israel. The situation seemed desperate. But the Jews of Israel fought with their backs to the wall, and triumphed over the huge Arab armies.

Since then about thirteen hundred thousand Jews from Europe, Asia, and Africa have entered Israel. Great efforts are being made to reclaim the desert lands to provide food for the immigrants, and many industries have been established. The Jews of America extended, and continue to extend, generous financial and moral aid.

All this time, however, Israel had to be on constant guard against threats to her survival. The Arab countries had not made peace with her. For years, her borders were subjected to raids from Arab infiltrators based in Egypt, particularly in the Gaza Strip. On October 29, 1956, Israel struck back, conquering the Gaza Strip and the Sinai Peninsula in a swift operation that lasted just four days. Captured documents and arms supplies revealed that the Gaza Strip had been readied as a springboard for an Egyptian invasion of Israel. But several months later Israel withdrew her troops from the Gaza Strip and and the Sinai Peninsula at the request of the United Nations.

Beginning late in 1966 Israel's border settlements were increasingly harassed by raids from Arab infiltrators based in Jordan and Syria. In the Spring of 1967 Egypt, Jordan and Syria mobilized for an all-out Arab attack against Israel. After getting the United Nations to withdraw the peace-keeping forces that had been stationed in the Sinai Peninsula and in the Gaza Strip since the war of 1956, and signing a mutual defense pact with Jordan, Egypt's President Abdel Gamel Nasser blockaded the port of Elath, Israel's outlet to the Gulf of Aqaba and the Red Sea.

In the morning of June 5, 1967, Israel retaliated, destroying most of the Arab air force on the ground within hours. With the skies clear of enemy planes, Israel's army was able to move ahead swiftly, occupying the Gaza Strip and the Sinai Peninsula, and reaching the eastern bank of the Suez Canal within eighty-nine hours. When Jordan opened fire on the Israeli sector of Jerusalem, Israel's troops thrust deep into Jordan, occupying the Jordanian sector west of the River Jordan. After three days of fighting, the Old City of Jerusalem was in Israeli hands, and, for the first time in two thousand years, the Wailing Wall was under Jewish control.

Israel next sent her troops into Syria and captured Syrian fortifications in the Golan hills from which the Syrians had been shelling Israeli settlements in the Galilee.

The outbreak of this war set off unprecedented demonstrations of solidarity from world Jewry. Millions of dollars were raised within hours to aid the Israeli war effort, and hundreds of Jews from all over the western world volunteered their services to Israel. But before these volunteers could arrive in Israel in large numbers the fighting was all but over. The entire war had lasted only six days.

WORLD JEWRY TODAY

At the present time there exist only two large Jewish centers in the world — one in the English speaking countries, and the other in Israel. The third large community, in Russia, is cut off from all contact with the rest of the world by an impenetrable curtain, and is being subjected to a policy of religious and cultural obliteration. Smaller but significant Jewish communities exist in some of the Latin American countries. The Jewish communities in Arab lands have greatly decreased in population. Algeria, for instance, which had 120,000 Jews in 1961, now has no more than 2,000.

A continued close relationship between the Jews of Israel and those living in the rest of the free world should hold out much promise for the spiritual and cultural growth and enrichment of the Jewish people as a whole.

HIGHLIGHTS OF AMERICAN JEWISH HISTORY

The Discovery and Settlement of America

When Columbus set out in 1492 to find a short route to India, and discovered America instead, there were Marranos Jews secreted among the crews of his vessels. Jewish history in America thus begins with the history of America itself. Jews were among the first settlers in the New World.

It is recorded that secret synagogues existed in the New World in the 1500's. In 1630 the Netherlands occupied part of Brazil, and the Marranos living there openly returned to Judaism. About two thousand Jews from Europe also emigrated there, and the first free Jewish congregation in the New World was established in the city of Recife.

But the rule of the Netherlands did not last long. In 1654 the Portuguese drove the Dutch out of Brazil, and the Jews were forced to leave. Some went back to the home country, some to other Dutch colonies in America. A small group of twenty-three Jews sailed northward and reached New Amsterdam (now New York) in September, 1654.

The First Jewish Community in North America

Though individual Jews had lived in North America before 1654, those who came from Brazil constituted the first permanent Jewish settlement. At first the governor of New Amsterdam, Peter Stuyvesant, refused to let them stay. They appealed to the Dutch West India Company, in whose behalf Stuyvesant governed, and obtained a Grant of Privileges to live and trade there. Within two years they also obtained the rights to travel, to own houses, to maintain a cemetery, and other privileges. But though they held services in homes, they were not granted the right to establish a synagogue. It was only in 1664, when New Amsterdam was annexed by England and renamed New York, that a declaration of religious freedom was issued, giving them the right to rent a house of worship for their congregation, which was named *Shearith Israel*.

The Spread of Jewish Settlement

Other Jewish communities soon came into existence. In 1658, fifteen Jewish families settled in Newport, Rhode Island. Jews came to Connecticut in 1659; to North Carolina in 1665; to Georgia in 1733.

Jewish immigration continued throughout the colonial period. It originated in England, Holland, Germany, Poland. The immigrants were traders, artisans, physicians. Wherever ten Jewish men (the quorum required for public worship, called a *minyan*) settled, they met to worship. They established cemeteries, and formed congregations. When their numbers increased, they built synagogues. In 1727, the congregation *Shearith Israel* built its first synagogue on Mill street.

Most of these early American Jews were Sefardim (decended from the Jews of Spain and Portugal). They clung devoutly to their faith, but did not segregate themselves socially, nor did their Christian neighbors shun them in any manner. The groundwork for the free American society that emerged later, was already being laid, and these early Jews actively participated in this society. They formed partnerships with their neighbors. There were Jewish students at the University of Pennsylvania in the 1760's. Jews accompanied George Washington in his expedition against the French. Ezra Stiles, President of Yale University, sought the company of Jewish scholars. He also studied Hebrew and visited the synagogue at Newport.

Hebrew Influence on Early America

Integration of the early Jews into the new American society was facilitated by a number of factors. The spirit of religious equality was strong in the land, because the country was being settled by various sects and denominations. The Puritans were deeply devoted to the Bible, and their ministers studied Hebrew. The Hebraic influence was so great, in fact, that at one time it was suggested that Hebrew be made the official language of the country.

The Revolutionary War

It was natural that the Jews should participate actively in the Revolutionary War that won independence for the United States. There were only about 2,000 Jews in the thirteen colonies at the time. Many Jews fought under Washington. Jewish merchants helped to raise funds to finance the war. The best known of these was Haym Salomon. George Washington took cognizance of Jewish aid in the cause of American independence, in letters of praise to various congregations.

Immigration from Central Europe

Jews from Central Europe came to America throughout the colonial period. At the time of the Revolution, these Jews, called Ashkenazim, already outnumbered the Sephardic Jews.

After 1815, when severe repressions set in, in Europe, German-speaking Jews began to arrive in ever increasing numbers. Of 6,000 Jews in the United States in 1826, more than three-quarters were Germans. In 1848 Central Europe experienced great political unrest which led to another tide of German-Jewish immigration. Many of these newcomers settled in the Middle West and Far West. At first they faced a hard struggle for existence. But soon they attained economic well-being, and contributed greatly to development of the frontier settlements. As traders, merchants, and artisans, they brought to outlying communities the comforts of civilization and higher standards of living.

The German-speaking Jews also developed an active Jewish life outside the synagogue. They established fraternal and literary societies, founding *Bnai Brith* with twelve members in 1843. Within a short time this order had thousands of members. Today it numbers hundreds of thousands. Other fraternal and benevolent organizations, such as the *Brith Abraham,* developed rapidly.

The German immigrants also established many congregations and synagogues. In 1825 they had only two; by 1848 there were seventy-seven synagogues throughout the country. Some also maintained Hebrew Schools for the children. However, many of the small communities lacked qualified teachers.

The Civil War

At the time of the Civil War, the Jewish population of the United States numbered nearly 200,000. Jews were active in national life. They participated in John Brown's revolt against slavery. They were among the founders of the Republican Party. Some also took a leading part on the side of the South. (Judah P. Banjamin was Secretary of State of the Confederate States.) About 6,000 Jews served in the Union ranks; another 1,200 wore the uniform of the Confederacy.

Rise of the Reform Movement

The period from 1850 to 1880 marked the peak of German Jewish immigration.

It is estimated that about 100,000 German Jews entered this country during that time.

This period also marked the rise of Reform Judaism in the United States. Most of the new arrivals were saturated with the spirit of religious change. With them came a number of rabbis who had been leaders of the movement in Germany. Outstanding among these was Isaac Meyer Wise (1819-1900). Rabbi Wise organized the Union of American Hebrew Congregations in 1873. He also founded in 1875 the *Hebrew Union College* at Cincinnati to train rabbis. The latter institution is now merged with the *Jewish Institute of Religion,* which was founded by Dr. Stephen S. Wise in 1922.

Achievements of German Jewish Immigrants

The German Jewish immigration, which shaped Jewish life in America through most of the nineteenth century, has many notable achievements to its credit. It built many charitable institutions, including the famed Mt. Sinai Hospital in New York. In 1859 the United Hebrew Charities was established. It organized large and influential fraternal and social orders. A thriving periodical press was established in both the German and English languages. At this time, too, American Jews began to take an active interest in the defense of persecuted Jewish communities abroad, as in the case of the blood libel against the Jews of Damascus, and persecutions in Switzerland and in the Papal States. Economic relief activities in Palestine were also undertaken.

Mordecai Emanuel Noah (1785-1851)

Mordecai Emanuel Noah, a distinguished journalist, active in this country's political life (he served as American consul in Tunis for several years), dreamed the age-old hope of the Jewish people: to overcome dispersion and oppression. In 1825 he undertook the ambitious project of establishing a Jewish state on Grand Island in the Niagara River, near the Falls. He bought the land, then still a wilderness, and wrote to Jewish communities in Europe to come make their home there. Inauguration of his project was celebrated in a church in Buffalo, New York, on September 2, 1825 He hoped that in time the small project on Grand Island might expand into the surrounding unsettled countryside, and provide a haven of safety for the Jews of Europe. But his appeals remained unanswered.

The New Immigration from Eastern Europe

In 1881-1882, and again in 1905, waves of bloody pogroms swept the Jewish

HEBREW UNION COLLEGE, CINCINNATI, OHIO — REFORM

communities in Czarist Russia. This persecution gave rise to the vast Jewish migration from East Europe. There were only about 250,000 Jews in the United States in 1880. By the time this mass immigration was virtually halted as a result of racist laws in 1924, the Jewish community had grown to four and a half million.

These newcomers, Yiddish-speaking, faced difficult conditions. They worked in factories, where they had to labor long hours for meager wages. Conditions in these establishments were so bad that they came to be known as "sweatshops." Economically poor, and forlorn in their new environment, the immigrants crowded into slums.

However, they enjoyed some important advantages. They brought with them a rich cultural heritage of learning and tradition. They were self-reliant, had a keen sense of responsibility for Jews overseas, and a strong feeling for social justice. They cherished a great love for America, which had given them freedom and opportunity after the persecutions suffered in Eastern Europe.

The Eastern Jews established schools and academies. They organized self-help institutions, labor and fraternal orders and *Landsmannschaften* (organizations of persons from the same town in the Old Country).

Many political educational and social movements aiming to improve the lot of Jews, and of humanity in general, grew popular. Zionism, socialism, and other nationalist and political trends had wide followings in the crowded immigrant districts. They also organized themselves into labor unions to fight for better working conditions. Within a relatively short time they achieved many of their economic goals, and the sweatshops became a thing of the past.

The Yiddish Press and Literature

Unlike the Jewish immigrants of the eighteenth and early nineteenth centuries, those who came from Eastern Europe clung to the Yiddish language. The first Yiddish weekly magazine appeared in 1885. Later a number of Yiddish dailies were established. The most influential of these, The *Jewish Daily Forward,* and *The Day — Jewish Morning Journal,* have a large number of readers to this day. These periodicals helped the immigrants in many ways. The Yiddish press helped preserve the cultural values the immigrants had brought with them; it imparted American culture and ways of life, and led them to higher standards of living.

In addition to newspapers and magazines, an extensive literature in Yiddish was produced in the United States. Poets, novelists, story writers, and dramatists produced important works, many of which were to be translated into English.

The Hebrew Press and Literature

A Hebrew press and literature also developed, though on a smaller scale than Yiddish. At one time a Hebrew daily was published in New York. Since Hebrew was not the spoken language of the masses, its use was largely restricted to literature, education, and religion. At present Hebrew is gaining in popularity, with numerous Hebrew schools and the introduction of the study into many high schools, colleges, and universities. There are also a number of Hebrew periodicals in America. *Hadoar,* now over thirty years old, is the only Hebrew weekly outside Israel.

Relief Agencies.

The Jewish immigrants felt responsibility for the welfare of Jews throughout the world. There evolved organizations and institutions whose chief purpose was to aid needy Jews abroad and recent arrivals in this country. In 1898 *HIAS* (Hebrew Sheltering and Immigrant Aid Society) was founded. For more than fifty years this organization helped thousands of immigrants overcome their difficulties of adjustment to the new circumstances. During World War I, when Jews in Europe suffered great hardship, the American Jewish Joint Distribution Committee (J.D.C.) was established. This organization has been carrying on its work since 1914 in many countries. At this time it is most active in North Africa and Israel. When refugees from German persecution began to arrive in this country, the United Service for New Americans was established to help them during their first years.

Educational Institutions

As the mass of immigrants settled down and began to feel more at home, they devoted themselves to their educational and spiritual needs. *The Jewish Theological Seminary,* which trains rabbis for conservative synagogues, was established in 1886, and it has been expanding its activities ever since. In 1896 the *Rabbi Isaac Elchanan Theological Seminary* was founded in New York to train orthodox rabbis. This institution is now *Yeshiva University,* with graduate, medical, and other colleges.

THE JEWISH THEOLOGICAL SEMINARY OF AMERICA, NEW YORK CITY — CONSERVATIVE

In 1907 a post-graduate institution known as the *Dropsie College for Hebrew and Cognate Learning* was established in Philadelphia, and in 1948 *Brandeis University* was founded in Massachusetts as a non-sectarian school under Jewish auspices. Hebrew Teachers Colleges have been established in New York, Chicago, Philadelphia, Boston, Baltimore, and other cities.

Schools employing Yiddish, Hebrew, and English have multiplied. During the past fifteen years many *all-day* Jewish schools have come into existence; in the *all-day* schools, religious and secular subjects are taught in the curriculum.

Recent Trends

Though thousands of new Jewish immigrants came to the United States after World War II, the vast majority of American Jews, who today number over five million, are the children and grandchildren of immigrants who arrived in this country before 1924. Many changes have taken place in American Jewry during the past three decades, and American Jews of today differ in many respects from the previous generation.

For one thing, English is now the spoken language of all American Jews, opening new avenues for cultural development. Scores of Anglo-Jewish periodicals and innumerable books in English on Jewish subjects are being published.

Personal ties with Jews in the Old Country have been virtually ended. This would have happened naturally in the course of time, but the complete severance came about suddenly as the result of the extermination of European Jewry by the Nazis. Some *Landsmannschaften* were held together by common interest in the welfare of the Jewish communities in their native towns. Now most of these East European communities have been wiped out.

YESHIVA UNIVERSITY, NEW YORK CITY — ORTHODOX

As the economic condition of the Jewish immigrant workers improved, they gave their children a higher education, taking advantage of the unlimited educational opportunities here, and satisfying the age-old Jewish love of learning. Large numbers also left the factories and went into business. As a result of these processes, the number of Jewish factory workers has decreased, while the percentage of Jewish businessmen, professionals, and scientists has grown.

Three Hundred Years

America is a land of pioneering. Jews have made great contributions to American achievement.

Jews pioneered in philanthropy, and set the pattern for the Community Chest movement. They introduced free loans, cooperative credit, settlement work, and similar services.

Jewish workers were pioneers in trade unionism, in unemployment insurance, cooperative housing, labor banking. Jews rank among the foremost American labor leaders. Together with Jewish industrialists, Jewish Labor often set the pattern for peaceful settlement of disputes by arbitration.

Jewish enterprise pioneered and developed the garment industry in this country, as well as motion pictures and plastics. Jews have also scored notable advances in scientific discovery, and in scholastic and literary work.

At the end of three hundred years of organized community existence in America, Jews can look with pride to their past achievements and with hope to the future. The most difficult periods of adjustment are behind them. Communal life is well organized and capable of meeting problems as they arise. American Jews have struck deep roots in the soil of the New World. Together with all other Americans they are eager to work for the further progress of their country. But in the midst of their prosperity they have not lost sight of that destiny which they share with Jews throughout the world. There is still a brotherhood among all — not political, but religious, cultural, and philanthropic.

STATUE OF LIBERTY, IN NEW YORK HARBOR
Presented to the United States by the people of France in 1884.

On the base of the statue are the following words, a sonnet by Emma Lazarus:

THE NEW COLOSSUS

Not like the brazen giant of Greek fame,
With conquering limbs astride from land to land,
Here at our sea-washing, sunset gates shall stand
A mighty woman with a torch, whose flame
Is the imprisoned lightning, and her name
Mother of Exiles. From her beacon hand
Glows world-wide welcome; her mild eyes command
The air-bridged harbor that twin cities frame.
"Keep, ancient lands, your storied pomp!"
    cries she
With silent lips. "Give me your tired, your poor,
Your huddled masses, yearning to breathe free,
The wretched refuse of your teeming shore.
Send these, the homeless, tempest-tossed, to me.
I lift my lamp beside the golden door!"